Easy Offer

The Python Interview Playbook

Ace Every Question with Confidence

Konstantin Ryabichenko

Copyright Page

ISBN: 9798345872864

Published by: Amazon Kindle Direct Publishing (KDP)

First Edition: October 2024

Contents

Acknowledgments

I would like to express my deepest gratitude to everyone who supported me throughout the work on this book. Without your help, inspiration, and encouragement, this project would not have been possible.

Thank you to my team and colleagues, with whom I shared my experience, and who helped make the material in the book more practical and useful for readers. Your advice and recommendations played a crucial role in creating this book.

A special thanks to my friends and loved ones for their patience and understanding. Your constant encouragement and belief in me helped me move forward, even when things were difficult.

And, of course, I am grateful to all the readers of this book. I hope it becomes a valuable resource for you and helps you on your path to new professional successes.

Sincerely,
Konstantin Ryabichenko

Introduction

Key Features That Make Python Popular Among Developers

Python's popularity among developers can be attributed to several key features that make it both beginner-friendly and powerful for advanced users:

1. **Simplicity and Readability**: Python's syntax is designed to be clean and easy to read, making it an excellent choice for beginners and a favorite among professionals who value clarity. The language promotes the use of whitespace for code blocks, which helps maintain readability.

2. **Extensive Standard Library**: Python comes with a comprehensive standard library that includes modules and packages for web development, file handling, data manipulation, and more. This makes it possible to accomplish a wide range of tasks without the need for third-party libraries.

3. **Cross-Platform Compatibility**: Python is available on major operating systems like Windows, macOS, and Linux. This cross-platform compatibility allows developers to write code once and run it anywhere.

4. **Versatile Ecosystem**: Python boasts a rich ecosystem of third-party libraries and frameworks, including:

   - **Web Development**: Django, Flask, FastAPI.

   - **Data Science**: NumPy, pandas, scikit-learn, TensorFlow.

   - **Automation**: Selenium, BeautifulSoup, PyAutoGUI.

5. **Active Community and Support**: Python has one of the largest and most active programming communities. There are countless forums, discussion groups, and open-source projects where developers can seek help, share knowledge, and contribute to the language's growth.

6. **Integration Capabilities**: Python's flexibility makes it easy to integrate with other languages (like C, C++, and Java) and technologies, making it a powerful tool for diverse development environments.

Why Python Is a Top Choice for Web Development, Data Science, and Automation

Python's dominance in several fields is no coincidence—it's a result of its adaptability and powerful features:

Web Development

Python's frameworks, such as Django and Flask, simplify the development of web applications by providing tools for URL routing, database handling, user authentication, and templating. These frameworks follow the "Don't Repeat Yourself" (DRY) principle, encouraging reusable code and modular development.

Data Science and Machine Learning

Python's data-handling capabilities are unmatched, making it the go-to language for data scientists. Libraries like pandas, NumPy, and Matplotlib enable quick data analysis, while scikit-learn and TensorFlow provide tools for building and training machine learning models. Python's ease of use allows data scientists to focus on solving complex problems rather than struggling with code.

Automation and Scripting

Python excels in automating repetitive tasks. Whether it's file manipulation, web scraping, or system administration, Python scripts can save time and reduce human error. The language's simple syntax, combined with modules like os, shutil, and subprocess, makes Python a powerful tool for automation.

How to Use This Book for Interview Preparation

This book is structured to help you prepare for Python developer interviews at different levels: Junior, Middle, and Senior. Here's how to make the most out of it:

1. **Chapter Structure**: Each chapter is dedicated to a specific topic or concept, starting with basic questions for beginners and progressing to more advanced questions for experienced developers.

2. **Code Examples**: The book includes code examples to illustrate key concepts and best practices. Study these examples carefully and try to replicate them on your own development environment.

3. **Practice Problems**: After reading each section, practice solving similar problems. Rewriting code and experimenting with variations will solidify your understanding.

4. **Mock Interview Tips**: Use the Q&A format to practice explaining concepts out loud, as you would in a real interview. Being able to articulate your thoughts clearly is just as important as having technical knowledge.

5. **Highlighting Key Concepts**: Pay attention to common pitfalls and frequently asked interview questions. These are highlighted to help you focus on areas that are commonly tested during interviews.

Preparing for Python Developer Interviews (Junior, Middle, Senior Levels)

Interview preparation varies depending on the level you are targeting. Here's a quick overview of what to expect at each level:

Junior Level

For junior roles, companies focus on assessing your foundational knowledge and ability to work with basic Python concepts. Expect questions related to:

- Basic syntax and operations
- Data types, variables, and control structures
- File handling and simple data processing
- Fundamental object-oriented programming concepts
- Basic debugging and problem-solving skills

Middle Level

At this level, interviewers will test your ability to write efficient and maintainable code, along with a deeper understanding of Python:

- Advanced data structures and algorithms
- Intermediate object-oriented programming (OOP)
- Functional programming and design patterns
- Database interactions (SQL and NoSQL)
- RESTful APIs and web frameworks like Flask and Django
- Unit testing and code coverage

Senior Level

Senior Python developer interviews focus on your ability to solve complex problems, design scalable systems, and demonstrate leadership:

- In-depth knowledge of OOP and metaprogramming

- Performance optimization and profiling

- Memory management and concurrency (multithreading, asynchronous programming)

- Design patterns and architectural principles

- Distributed systems and microservices

- Security best practices and deployment strategies

- Team collaboration and project leadership

By understanding what is expected at each level, you can tailor your preparation accordingly. This book is designed to guide you step-by-step through all these concepts, ensuring you are well-prepared for any Python developer interview

Section 1: Basic Questions

1.1 Introduction to Python

What Is Python, and What Are Its Key Features?

Python is a high-level, interpreted programming language known for its simplicity and versatility. It was created by Guido van Rossum and first released in 1991. Python is designed to emphasize code readability with its clean and straightforward syntax, making it easy for beginners to learn and for experienced developers to work with.

Key Features of Python:

1. **Readability and Simplicity**: Python's syntax is intuitive and closely resembles English, which allows developers to write clear and concise code. This makes it easier to read, maintain, and debug.

2. **Interpreted Language**: Python code is executed line-by-line by the Python interpreter, which means you can test code quickly without needing a compilation step. This supports rapid development and debugging.

3. **Dynamic Typing**: You don't need to declare variable types explicitly. Python automatically assigns the type at runtime, which allows for more flexible and concise code.

   ```python
   x = 10       # Integer
   x = "Hello"  # String, variable type changes dynamically
   ```

4. **Large Standard Library**: Python comes with a vast library of modules and packages, covering everything from web development (Django, Flask) to data analysis (NumPy, pandas) and system administration (os, shutil).

5. **Cross-Platform Compatibility**: Python runs on Windows, macOS, and Linux without any modification, making it a powerful choice for multi-platform development.

6. **Object-Oriented and Functional Programming**: Python supports both object-oriented and functional programming paradigms, giving developers the flexibility to choose the best approach for their projects.

7. **Community Support**: Python has a large, active community that contributes to a rich ecosystem of third-party libraries and tools. This provides ample resources for problem-solving, code examples, and documentation

.

8

What Is the Difference Between Python 2.x and Python 3.x?

Python 3.x was introduced in 2008 to address fundamental design flaws and improve the language. It is not backward-compatible with Python 2.x, which reached end-of-life in 2020. Here are the primary differences between Python 2.x and Python 3.x:

Feature	Python 2.x	Python 3.x
Print Statement	print "Hello World"	print("Hello World")
Integer Division	5 / 2 results in 2	5 / 2 results in 2.5
Unicode Support	Strings are ASCII by default	Strings are Unicode by default
Error Handling	except Exception, e: syntax	except Exception as e: syntax
Library Compatibility	Many libraries support 2.x only	New libraries are 3.x only
iteritems() in Dictionaries	dict.iteritems()	dict.items()

Python 3.x brings enhanced features like improved syntax, Unicode support, and better performance. New projects should always use Python 3.x.

How Does Python's Interpreter Work?

Python is an interpreted language, meaning that code is executed line-by-line using an interpreter rather than being compiled into machine code beforehand. Here's how Python's interpreter processes code:

1. **Lexical Analysis**: The interpreter reads the source code and converts it into tokens (the smallest elements like keywords, identifiers, operators).

2. **Parsing**: The interpreter analyzes the token stream to create a syntax tree (Abstract Syntax Tree or AST) that represents the code structure.

3. **Compilation**: The syntax tree is transformed into bytecode, an intermediate language that is platform-independent.

4. **Execution**: The bytecode is executed by the Python Virtual Machine (PVM), which interprets each bytecode instruction and interacts with the system's underlying hardware and operating system.

Here's a simple illustration of how Python executes code:

```
# Example of Python code
x = 5
y = 10
print(x + y)
```

The code above goes through the interpreter's steps, finally printing the result: 15.

What Are Python's Dynamic Typing and Strong Typing Features?

Dynamic Typing

Python is dynamically typed, meaning that variables do not have a fixed type. You can assign different types of data to the same variable without declaring its type:

```
x = 10      # x is an integer
x = "Python" # Now x is a string
```

Dynamic typing makes Python flexible, but it requires developers to be mindful of potential runtime errors.

Strong Typing

Python is also strongly typed, which means that it does not automatically convert data types when performing operations. An explicit conversion is required:

```
# Example of strong typing
x = "5"
y = 10
# print(x + y)  # This will cause a TypeError

# Corrected with explicit conversion
print(int(x) + y)  # Output: 15
```

How Do You Install and Set Up Python on Different Platforms (Windows, macOS, Linux)?

Python installation is straightforward across different platforms. Below are step-by-step instructions for setting up Python:

Windows

1. **Download**: Go to Python's official website and download the Windows installer for Python 3.x.

2. **Run the Installer**: Check the box that says "Add Python to PATH" during the installation.

3. **Verify the Installation**: Open Command Prompt and type:

```
python --version
```

4. **Install Packages**: Use pip, the Python package manager:

```
pip install requests
```

macOS

1. **Download**: Visit Python's official website and download the macOS installer.

2. **Install Using Homebrew** (Alternative): Open Terminal and run:

```
brew install python
```

3. **Verify Installation**: In Terminal, type:

```
python3 --version
```

4. **Install Packages**:

```
pip3 install requests
```

Linux

1. **Use the Package Manager**: Most Linux distributions come with Python pre-installed. To install the latest version:

   o **Debian/Ubuntu**:

   ```
   sudo apt update
   sudo apt install python3 python3-pip
   ```

   o **Fedora**:

   ```
   sudo dnf install python3
   ```

2. **Verify Installation**:

```
python3 --version
```

3. **Install Packages**:

```
pip3 install requests
```

What Is PEP 8, and Why Is It Important for Python Developers?

PEP 8 (Python Enhancement Proposal 8) is the official style guide for Python code. It provides guidelines and best practices for writing clean, readable, and consistent code. Adhering to PEP 8 helps maintain code quality and improves collaboration in teams. Key PEP 8 recommendations include:

1. **Indentation**: Use 4 spaces per indentation level.

2. **Line Length**: Keep lines of code under 79 characters.

3. **Naming Conventions**: Use snake_case for variables and functions, CamelCase for classes.

4. **Whitespace**: Avoid extra spaces within parentheses, brackets, or braces.

5. **Comments**: Use comments to explain complex sections of code, and keep them concise.

Example following PEP 8:

```python
# Good PEP 8 example
def calculate_sum(a, b):
    """Calculate the sum of two numbers."""
    return a + b
```

How Do You Check the Version of Python Installed on Your System?

To check which version of Python is installed on your system, use the command line:

Windows

Open Command Prompt and type:

```
python --version
```

or

```
python -V
```

macOS / Linux

Open Terminal and type:

```
python3 --version
```

or

```
python3 -V
```

Additionally, you can check the version from within a Python script:

```
import sys
print(sys.version)
```

The output will display the Python version along with additional build information.

1.2 Data Types and Variables

What Are Python's Built-In Data Types (e.g., int, float, str, bool, list, dict)?

Python supports a variety of built-in data types that allow developers to store and manipulate data efficiently. These data types can be broadly categorized as follows:

1. Numeric Types

- int: Represents whole numbers (e.g., 10, -5, 42).

- float: Represents floating-point numbers, which are numbers with a decimal point (e.g., 3.14, 0.001).

- complex: Represents complex numbers with a real and imaginary part (e.g., 2 + 3j).

2. Text Type

- str: Represents sequences of characters (e.g., "Hello, World!"). Strings in Python are immutable, meaning they cannot be modified after creation.

3. Boolean Type

- bool: Represents Boolean values (True or False). This is often used in control flow and conditional expressions.

4. Sequence Types

- **list**: An ordered, mutable (modifiable) collection of items (e.g., [1, 2, 3, "apple"]).

- **tuple**: An ordered, immutable collection of items (e.g., (1, 2, 3)).

5. Set Types

- **set**: An unordered collection of unique items (e.g., {1, 2, 3}). Sets do not allow duplicate elements and are mutable.

6. Mapping Type

- **dict**: A collection of key-value pairs (e.g., {"name": "Alice", "age": 25}). Dictionaries are mutable and allow fast lookups by key.

Example of Data Types in Python:

```python
# Numeric types
x = 10        # int
y = 3.14      # float
z = 2 + 3j    # complex

# Text type
greeting = "Hello, Python!"

# Boolean type
is_valid = True

# Sequence types
numbers = [1, 2, 3, 4]    # list
coordinates = (10, 20)    # tuple

# Set type
unique_numbers = {1, 2, 3, 4}

# Mapping type
person = {"name": "Alice", "age": 25}
```

How Are Variables Declared in Python Compared to Other Languages (e.g., Java, C++)?

In Python, variables are dynamically typed, meaning you don't have to declare their type explicitly, unlike in languages such as Java or C++. You simply assign a value to a variable, and Python determines the type based on that value.

Python Example:

```
x = 42          # Integer assignment
name = "Python"  # String assignment
price = 19.99    # Float assignment
```

Java Example:

```
int x = 42;
String name = "Java";
double price = 19.99;
```

C++ Example:

```
int x = 42;
std::string name = "C++";
double price = 19.99;
```

Key Differences:

1. **No Type Declaration**: In Python, you don't need to declare a variable's type. The interpreter infers the type at runtime.

2. **Dynamic Typing**: Variables can change types dynamically:

```
x = 10
x = "Now a string"   # No error, type changes dynamically
```

3. **No Special Syntax for Declarations**: Variables in Python are created the moment you first assign a value to them.

How Do You Manipulate Strings in Python (Concatenation, Slicing, Formatting)?

String Concatenation

You can concatenate strings using the + operator or by using f-strings (formatted string literals).

```python
# Using + operator
greeting = "Hello"
name = "Alice"
message = greeting + ", " + name + "!"
# Output: "Hello, Alice!"
# Using f-strings (Python 3.6+)
message = f"{greeting}, {name}!"
```

String Slicing

Strings in Python can be sliced using square brackets with the syntax string[start:end]. The start index is inclusive, and the end index is exclusive.

```python
text = "Python"
first_three = text[:3]     # Output: "Pyt"
last_three = text[-3:]     # Output: "hon"
reversed_text = text[::-1] # Output: "nohtyP"
```

String Formatting

Python provides several ways to format strings:

1. **% Formatting (Old-style)**:

    ```python
    name = "Alice"
    age = 30
    info = "Name: %s, Age: %d" % (name, age)
    ```

2. **str.format() Method**:

    ```python
    info = "Name: {}, Age: {}".format(name, age)
    ```

3. **f-strings (Recommended)**:

    ```python
    info = f"Name: {name}, Age: {age}"
    ```

How Do You Create, Access, and Modify Lists and Tuples in Python?

Creating Lists and Tuples

- **List**: A mutable sequence.

   ```
   fruits = ["apple", "banana", "cherry"]
   ```

- **Tuple**: An immutable sequence.

   ```
   coordinates = (10, 20)
   ```

Accessing Elements

You can access elements using an index. Lists and tuples use zero-based indexing.

```
# Accessing elements
first_fruit = fruits[0]    # "apple"
x, y = coordinates         # Unpacking tuples: x = 10, y = 20
```

Modifying Lists

Lists are mutable, so you can change, add, or remove elements.

```
# Modify list elements
fruits[1] = "blueberry"    # Change "banana" to "blueberry"
fruits.append("orange")    # Add "orange" to the end
del fruits[0]              # Remove "apple"
```

Tuples are Immutable

Once a tuple is created, its elements cannot be modified. You can, however, create a new tuple:

```
# Immutable nature of tuples
coordinates = (10, 20)
coordinates = (15, 25)   # Creates a new tuple
```

How Do You Use Sets in Python, and What Are Their Key Advantages?

A **set** is an unordered collection of unique elements. Sets are useful for performing operations like union, intersection, and difference efficiently. They are created using curly braces {} or the set() function.

Creating and Using Sets

```python
# Creating sets
numbers = {1, 2, 3, 4}
empty_set = set()  # Note: {} creates an empty dictionary, not a set
```

Key Advantages of Sets

1. **Uniqueness**: Sets automatically eliminate duplicate values.

   ```python
   numbers = {1, 2, 2, 3}  # Result: {1, 2, 3}
   ```

2. **Efficient Membership Testing**: Checking if an element is in a set is faster than in a list.

   ```python
   if 3 in numbers:
       print("3 is in the set")
   ```

3. **Mathematical Operations**: Sets support operations like union (|), intersection (&), and difference (-).

   ```python
   A = {1, 2, 3}
   B = {3, 4, 5}
   print(A | B)  # Union: {1, 2, 3, 4, 5}
   print(A & B)  # Intersection: {3}
   print(A - B)  # Difference: {1, 2}
   ```

What Is a Dictionary in Python, and How Do You Perform Key-Based Operations?

A **dictionary** is a mutable, unordered collection of key-value pairs. Keys must be unique and immutable, while values can be of any type.

Creating and Accessing a Dictionary

```python
# Creating a dictionary
person = {
    "name": "Alice",
    "age": 30,
    "city": "New York"
}
```

```
# Accessing values
print(person["name"])   # Output: Alice

# Using get() method to avoid KeyError
age = person.get("age", "Unknown")   # Output: 30
```

Modifying a Dictionary

Dictionaries are mutable, so you can add, update, or delete key-value pairs.

```
# Adding a new key-value pair
person["job"] = "Developer"

# Updating an existing value
person["age"] = 31

# Deleting a key-value pair
del person["city"]
```

How Do You Use Type Hinting in Python 3.x?

Type hinting, introduced in Python 3.5, allows developers to specify the expected data types for variables, function parameters, and return values. This does not enforce the type but helps improve code readability, provides better documentation, and supports static analysis tools like **mypy** for type checking.

Basic Type Hinting

You can use type hints for variables to indicate the intended type:

```
# Type hints for variables
name: str = "Alice"
age: int = 30
pi: float = 3.14159
is_active: bool = True
```

Function Annotations

Type hints are commonly used in function definitions to specify the expected parameter types and the return type:

```
# Function with type hints
def greet(name: str) -> str:
    return f"Hello, {name}!"

# Type hints for multiple parameters
def add_numbers(x: int, y: int) -> int:
    return x + y
```

In the example above:

- name: str indicates that the parameter name should be a string.

- -> str specifies that the function will return a string.

Type Hinting with Complex Data Structures

You can use type hints for complex data structures like lists, dictionaries, and custom types using the typing module.

```
from typing import List, Dict, Tuple

# Type hints for lists and dictionaries
names: List[str] = ["Alice", "Bob", "Charlie"]
ages: Dict[str, int] = {"Alice": 30, "Bob": 25}

# Function with list and tuple type hints
def process_data(data: List[int], threshold: int) -> Tuple[int, int]:
    above_threshold = [x for x in data if x > threshold]
    return len(above_threshold), sum(above_threshold)
```

In the example:

- List[str] indicates a list of strings.

- Dict[str, int] specifies a dictionary with string keys and integer values.

- Tuple[int, int] indicates a tuple containing two integers.

Type Hinting for Optional and Union Types

Sometimes, a function parameter might accept multiple types or be optional. The typing module provides Union and Optional for these scenarios:

```python
from typing import Union, Optional

# Union allows multiple types
def process_input(value: Union[int, float, str]) -> str:
    return f"Processed: {value}"

# Optional indicates that a value can be of a type or None
def find_user(user_id: Optional[int] = None) -> str:
    if user_id is None:
        return "No user found"
    return f"User ID: {user_id}"
```

Type Aliases and Custom Types

To simplify complex type definitions, you can create type aliases or define custom types using the NewType from the typing module:

```python
from typing import List, NewType

# Creating a type alias
Vector = List[float]

def calculate_magnitude(vector: Vector) -> float:
    return sum(x**2 for x in vector) ** 0.5

# Creating a custom type
UserID = NewType('UserID', int)

def get_user_name(user_id: UserID) -> str:
    return f"User with ID: {user_id}"
```

Advantages of Using Type Hinting

1. **Improved Readability**: Code with type hints is easier to understand since it documents expected types explicitly.

2. **Error Detection**: Tools like **mypy** can perform static type checking, helping to catch potential errors early in the development cycle.

3. **Editor Support**: Many modern IDEs provide better autocompletion, code suggestions, and warnings when using type hints.

4. **Documentation**: Type hints serve as built-in documentation for functions and modules, making it easier for other developers to understand the code.

Enforcing Type Checking with mypy

Although Python is dynamically typed, you can enforce stricter type checking using the mypy tool. This tool analyzes code based on the provided type hints to identify potential type errors.

1. **Install mypy:**

```
pip install mypy
```

2. **Run mypy on a Python file:**

```
mypy your_script.py
```

mypy will check if the types match the specified type hints and provide warnings if it detects any inconsistencies.

1.3 Control Flow and Iteration

How Do You Implement Conditional Statements (if, elif, else) in Python?

Conditional statements in Python allow you to execute certain blocks of code based on the evaluation of conditions. The most common conditional statements are if, elif (short for "else if"), and else.

Syntax Example:

```python
# Basic if-elif-else structure
x = 10

if x > 10:
    print("x is greater than 10")
elif x == 10:
    print("x is exactly 10")
else:
    print("x is less than 10")
```

Explanation:

- if: Checks a condition. If True, the code block indented under if is executed.

- elif: Provides additional conditions if the previous if was False.

- else: Executes if none of the preceding conditions were True.

Conditional Expressions (Ternary Operator)

Python also supports a shorthand form known as a conditional expression or a ternary operator:

```python
# Ternary operator example
age = 20
message = "Adult" if age >= 18 else "Minor"
print(message)  # Output: "Adult"
```

What Is the Difference Between for Loops and while Loops in Python?

Python provides two primary looping constructs: for loops and while loops.

for Loops

A for loop iterates over a sequence (like a list, tuple, string, or range) for a fixed number of iterations.

```python
# Example of a for loop
fruits = ["apple", "banana", "cherry"]

for fruit in fruits:
    print(fruit)
```

while Loops

A while loop continues to execute as long as a specified condition remains True. It is useful for loops where the number of iterations isn't known beforehand.

```python
# Example of a while loop
count = 0

while count < 5:
    print(f"Count is: {count}")
    count += 1
```

Key Differences:

1. `for` **loop**: Ideal for iterating over a collection or a range where the number of iterations is known.

2. `while` **loop**: Ideal for loops that need to continue until a specific condition is met.

How Do You Use List, Set, and Dictionary Comprehensions to Create Collections?

Comprehensions provide a concise way to create collections in Python, allowing you to generate lists, sets, or dictionaries in a single line of code.

List Comprehension

Creates a new list by applying an expression to each item in an existing iterable.

```python
# Example: Creating a list of squares
squares = [x**2 for x in range(10)]
# Output: [0, 1, 4, 9, 16, 25, 36, 49, 64, 81]

# With a condition
even_squares = [x**2 for x in range(10) if x % 2 == 0]
# Output: [0, 4, 16, 36, 64]
```

Set Comprehension

Similar to list comprehension but produces a set with unique elements.

```python
# Example: Creating a set of unique squares
unique_squares = {x**2 for x in [1, 2, 2, 3, 4, 4]}
# Output: {1, 4, 9, 16}
```

Dictionary Comprehension

Creates a new dictionary by applying an expression to each item.

```python
# Example: Creating a dictionary with numbers as keys and their squares
as values
square_dict = {x: x**2 for x in range(5)}
# Output: {0: 0, 1: 1, 2: 4, 3: 9, 4: 16}
```

How Do You Use break, continue, and pass in Loops?

Python provides break, continue, and pass statements to control the flow of loops.

break Statement

Exits the current loop entirely, skipping the remaining iterations.

```python
# Example: Using break to exit a loop
for num in range(10):
    if num == 5:
        break
    print(num)
# Output: 0, 1, 2, 3, 4
```

continue Statement

Skips the current iteration and moves to the next one.

```python
# Example: Using continue to skip certain numbers
for num in range(10):
    if num % 2 == 0:
        continue
    print(num)
# Output: 1, 3, 5, 7, 9
```

pass Statement

Does nothing and is often used as a placeholder for future code. It can be used to define an empty loop or function.

```python
# Example: Using pass as a placeholder
for _ in range(5):
    pass  # No operation, placeholder for future code
```

How Does Python Handle Nested Loops?

Python supports nested loops, meaning you can have a loop inside another loop. The inner loop will complete all its iterations for each iteration of the outer loop.

```python
# Example of nested loops
for i in range(3):     # Outer loop
```

```
    for j in range(2):   # Inner Loop
        print(f"i: {i}, j: {j}")
```

Output:

```
i: 0, j: 0
i: 0, j: 1
i: 1, j: 0
i: 1, j: 1
i: 2, j: 0
i: 2, j: 1
```

Performance Note:

Be cautious with nested loops as they can significantly increase the time complexity of your code. A common example is the use of nested loops to handle matrix operations or multi-dimensional data.

What Is the Difference Between is and == in Python Comparisons?

In Python, is and == are both used for comparisons, but they serve different purposes:

== Operator (Equality)

- Compares the values of two objects to check if they are equal.

- Returns True if the values are the same, regardless of whether they are the same object in memory.

```
# Example of == comparison
a = [1, 2, 3]
b = [1, 2, 3]
print(a == b)   # Output: True (values are equal)
```

is Operator (Identity)

- Compares whether two references point to the same object in memory.

- Returns True if both variables refer to the same object.

```
# Example of is comparison
a = [1, 2, 3]
b = a
c = [1, 2, 3]
```

```
print(a is b)    # Output: True (b is a reference to the same object as a)
print(a is c)    # Output: False (c is a different object with the same
value)
```

Key Difference:

- Use == when comparing values.

- Use is when checking if two variables point to the same object (e.g., None comparison).

How Do You Use enumerate() and zip() for Looping Through Multiple Collections?

enumerate() Function

The enumerate() function adds a counter to an iterable, returning a tuple of the index and the item.

```
# Example of using enumerate
fruits = ["apple", "banana", "cherry"]

for index, fruit in enumerate(fruits):
    print(f"Index {index}: {fruit}")
# Output:
# Index 0: apple
# Index 1: banana
# Index 2: cherry
```

zip() Function

The zip() function combines two or more iterables into a single iterator of tuples. It's useful for iterating over multiple collections in parallel.

```
# Example of using zip
names = ["Alice", "Bob", "Charlie"]
ages = [25, 30, 35]
for name, age in zip(names, ages):
    print(f"{name} is {age} years old.")
# Output:
# Alice is 25 years old.
# Bob is 30 years old.
# Charlie is 35 years old.
```

Practical Use Case:

Combining enumerate() and zip() can be useful for keeping track of indexes while iterating over multiple lists.

```python
# Example combining enumerate and zip
colors = ["red", "green", "blue"]
for index, (name, color) in enumerate(zip(names, colors)):
    print(f"{index}: {name} likes {color} color.")
# Output:
# 0: Alice likes red color.
# 1: Bob likes green color.
# 2: Charlie likes blue color.
```

1.4 Functions and Scope

How Do You Define Functions in Python Using the def Keyword?

In Python, functions are defined using the def keyword followed by the function name and parentheses. Functions are a way to encapsulate code into reusable blocks, making programs more modular and maintainable.

Basic Function Definition

```python
def greet(name):
    """Function to greet the user by name."""
    print(f"Hello, {name}!")
```

Function with Return Value

You can use the return statement to return a result from a function:

```python
def add(a, b):
    """Function to add two numbers and return the result."""
    return a + b
# Calling the function
result = add(5, 3)
print(result)  # Output: 8
```

Key Points:

- Function names should be descriptive and follow Python's naming conventions (typically snake_case).

- Use a docstring (triple quotes) to provide a brief description of the function's purpose.

What Is the Difference Between Positional and Keyword Arguments?

Python functions can accept parameters as either **positional** or **keyword** arguments.

Positional Arguments

These are the most common type of arguments. They are passed to a function in the order in which they are defined.

```python
def describe_person(name, age):
    print(f"{name} is {age} years old.")

# Using positional arguments
describe_person("Alice", 30)   # Output: Alice is 30 years old.
```

Keyword Arguments

With keyword arguments, you specify the parameter's name along with its value. This allows you to pass arguments in any order.

```python
# Using keyword arguments
describe_person(age=25, name="Bob")   # Output: Bob is 25 years old.
```

Key Differences:

1. **Positional**: Order matters; you must pass arguments in the same order as defined.

2. **Keyword**: Order doesn't matter; you specify parameters by name.

What Are *args and **kwargs, and How Are They Used in Python Functions?

Python functions can accept a variable number of arguments using *args and **kwargs.

*args (Non-Keyword Arguments)

The *args parameter allows you to pass a variable number of positional arguments. It's useful when the number of arguments is not known in advance.

```python
def sum_numbers(*args):
    """Function to sum an arbitrary number of numbers."""
    return sum(args)
# Using *args
result = sum_numbers(1, 2, 3, 4)  # Output: 10
```

**kwargs (Keyword Arguments)

The **kwargs parameter allows you to pass a variable number of keyword arguments. It's useful when you want to handle named arguments dynamically.

```python
def print_info(**kwargs):
    """Function to print information from keyword arguments."""
    for key, value in kwargs.items():
        print(f"{key}: {value}")
# Using **kwargs
print_info(name="Alice", age=30, job="Developer")
# Output:
# name: Alice
# age: 30
# job: Developer
```

Combining *args and **kwargs

You can use both *args and **kwargs together in the same function to accept both positional and keyword arguments.

```python
def full_description(name, *traits, **details):
    print(f"Name: {name}")
    print("Traits:", ", ".join(traits))
    for key, value in details.items():
        print(f"{key}: {value}")
# Example usage
full_description("Alice", "smart", "creative", age=30, job="Developer")
# Output:
# Name: Alice
# Traits: smart, creative
# age: 30
# job: Developer
```

How Do You Use Default Parameters in Function Definitions?

Python allows you to define default values for parameters in a function. If the caller does not provide a value for that parameter, the default value is used.

Example: Default Parameters

```python
def greet(name, greeting="Hello"):
    """Function with a default parameter."""
    print(f"{greeting}, {name}!")

# Calling with both arguments
greet("Alice", "Hi")  # Output: Hi, Alice!

# Calling with only the required argument
greet("Bob")  # Output: Hello, Bob!
```

Key Points:

- Default parameters should always be listed after non-default parameters.

- Default values are evaluated once when the function is defined, not each time it's called.

How Does Python Handle Variable Scope (Local, Global, Nonlocal)?

Python has different levels of variable scope that determine where variables can be accessed or modified:

1. **Local Scope**

   Variables defined inside a function are local to that function and cannot be accessed outside of it.

   ```python
   def example():
       x = 10  # Local variable
       print(x)

   example()  # Output: 10
   # print(x)  # Error: x is not defined outside the function
   ```

2. **Global Scope**

   Variables defined outside of any function are global and accessible throughout the script.

```
x = 20   # Global variable

def show():
    print(x)   # Accessing the global variable

show()   # Output: 20
```

To modify a global variable inside a function, use the global keyword:

```
x = 10
def modify_global():
    global x
    x = 30   # Modifies the global x
modify_global()
print(x)   # Output: 30
```

3. **Nonlocal Scope**

The nonlocal keyword is used in nested functions to refer to variables defined in the nearest enclosing scope (but not global).

```
def outer():
    x = 5

    def inner():
        nonlocal x
        x = 10   # Modifies x in the outer function scope

    inner()
    print(x)

outer()   # Output: 10
```

Scope Levels Order: Python resolves variable names using the LEGB rule:

- Local

- Enclosing

- Global

- Built-i

32

What Are Anonymous Functions (Lambdas), and When Should You Use Them?

Anonymous functions in Python are defined using the lambda keyword. They are small, one-line functions that do not have a name. Unlike regular functions, lambda functions can only have a single expression.

Syntax Example:

```python
# Regular function
def add(x, y):
    return x + y

# Equivalent lambda function
add = lambda x, y: x + y

# Using the lambda
result = add(3, 5)   # Output: 8
```

When to Use Lambdas:

1. **Small, Simple Operations**: Use lambdas for small functions that are easy to understand, typically passed as arguments to higher-order functions.

2. **Single Use**: Ideal when the function is needed only temporarily, such as sorting or filtering data.

Examples of Lambda Usage:

```python
# Sorting a list of tuples by the second element
pairs = [(1, 'one'), (2, 'two'), (3, 'three')]
pairs.sort(key=lambda x: x[1])

# Filtering even numbers from a list
numbers = [1, 2, 3, 4, 5, 6]
even_numbers = list(filter(lambda x: x % 2 == 0, numbers))   # Output:
[2, 4, 6]
```

How Do You Handle Recursion in Python?

Recursion is a technique where a function calls itself to solve smaller instances of a problem until it reaches a base case. Python supports recursion, but it's essential to have a base case to prevent infinite recursion.

Example: Factorial Calculation Using Recursion

```python
def factorial(n):
    """Calculates the factorial of a number using recursion."""
    if n == 0 or n == 1:  # Base case
        return 1
    else:
        return n * factorial(n - 1)

# Calling the recursive function
result = factorial(5)  # Output: 120
```

Key Points for Recursion:

1. **Base Case**: Ensure the function has a base case to stop recursion.

2. **Recursive Call**: Function should call itself with a modified argument to reduce the problem size.

3. **Performance Consideration**: Recursive functions can lead to a stack overflow if the recursion depth is too large. Use sys.setrecursionlimit() to change the recursion depth limit, but handle it carefully.

4. **Use Iterative Approach When Possible**: In some cases, iterative solutions may be more efficient than recursion due to Python's limited recursion depth.

Example: Fibonacci Sequence Using Recursion

```python
def fibonacci(n):
    """Calculates the nth Fibonacci number using recursion."""
    if n <= 1:  # Base cases
        return n
    else:
        return fibonacci(n - 1) + fibonacci(n - 2)

# Calculating the 6th Fibonacci number
result = fibonacci(6)  # Output: 8
```

1.5 Exception Handling

What Is Exception Handling, and Why Is It Important in Python?

Exception Handling is a mechanism in Python that allows you to manage runtime errors in a controlled way. Instead of causing the program to crash, exceptions can be caught and handled, allowing the program to continue or terminate gracefully. This is crucial for building robust and error-tolerant applications.

Why Is It Important?

1. **Improved User Experience**: Prevents programs from crashing unexpectedly, providing users with meaningful error messages or alternative actions.

2. **Debugging**: Helps identify where an error occurred, making it easier to debug and maintain code.

3. **Error Recovery**: Allows the program to handle errors gracefully, retry operations, or perform cleanup tasks.

4. **Resource Management**: Ensures resources like files or database connections are properly closed, even if an error occurs.

Basic Example:

```python
try:
    result = 10 / 0  # This will raise a ZeroDivisionError
except ZeroDivisionError:
    print("Error: Cannot divide by zero.")
```

In this example, a ZeroDivisionError is raised, but instead of crashing the program, the error is caught and handled by the except block.

How Do You Use try, except, else, and finally Blocks?

Python provides several keywords for handling exceptions in a structured way:

- **try Block**

  The code that might raise an exception goes inside the try block.

- **except Block**

  The code to handle the exception goes inside the except block. You can specify the type of exception you want to catch.

- **else Block**

  The else block runs if no exceptions were raised in the try block.

- **finally Block**

  The finally block always executes, whether an exception was raised or not. It's typically used for cleanup actions like closing files or releasing resources.

Syntax Example:

```python
try:
    # Code that might raise an exception
    number = int(input("Enter a number: "))
except ValueError:
    # Handles the specific exception
    print("That's not a valid number.")
else:
    # Executes if no exceptions were raised
    print(f"You entered: {number}")
finally:
    # Always executes, useful for cleanup
    print("Execution completed.")
```

Flow Explanation:

1. try: Attempt to execute the code.

2. except: Handle specific exceptions if they occur.

3. else: Run code if the try block was successful.

4. finally: Execute cleanup code regardless of success or failure.

What Is the Difference Between Syntax Errors and Exceptions in Python?

Syntax Errors

- These are errors in the structure of the code, detected by the interpreter before the code is executed.

- Syntax errors indicate mistakes in Python syntax, like missing colons, parentheses, or incorrect indentation.

- **Example**:

```
if True
    print("Missing colon")  # SyntaxError: invalid syntax
```

Exceptions

- These are errors detected during execution (runtime errors), even if the syntax is correct.

- Examples include ZeroDivisionError, ValueError, and FileNotFoundError.

- **Example**:

```
result = 10 / 0  # ZeroDivisionError: division by zero
```

Key Difference:

- **Syntax errors** must be corrected before the code can be executed.

- **Exceptions** occur during execution and can be handled using try-except blocks.

How Do You Use raise to Generate Custom Exceptions?

The raise keyword allows you to manually trigger an exception in Python. This is useful when you want to enforce certain conditions or when specific errors occur in your code.

Syntax Example:

```
def check_age(age):
    if age < 0:
        raise ValueError("Age cannot be negative.")
    return f"Age is: {age}"
# Calling the function with an invalid value
try:
```

```
    check_age(-5)
except ValueError as e:
    print(e)  # Output: Age cannot be negative.
```

Key Points:

- raise is followed by an exception type (e.g., ValueError).

- You can add a custom error message for better context.

How Do You Handle Multiple Exceptions in One Block?

Python allows you to handle multiple exceptions using a single except block or separate except blocks for different exceptions.

Handling Multiple Exceptions in One Block

You can catch multiple exceptions using a single except block by specifying a tuple of exception types.

```
try:
    value = int(input("Enter a number: "))
    result = 10 / value
except (ValueError, ZeroDivisionError) as e:
    print(f"An error occurred: {e}")
```

Handling Multiple Exceptions with Different Blocks

If you want to handle each exception type differently, you can use multiple except blocks:

```
try:
    value = int(input("Enter a number: "))
    result = 10 / value
except ValueError:
    print("That's not a valid number.")
except ZeroDivisionError:
    print("Cannot divide by zero.")
```

Key Points:

- Use a tuple of exceptions for a single except block when the handling is the same.

- Use separate except blocks for different handling strategies.

38

How Do You Create and Use Custom Exception Classes?

Python allows you to create custom exception classes by inheriting from the built-in Exception class. Custom exceptions are useful when you want to define specific error types for your application.

Creating a Custom Exception

```python
# Define a custom exception class
class NegativeAgeError(Exception):
    """Exception raised for negative age input."""
    def __init__(self, age, message="Age cannot be negative."):
        self.age = age
        self.message = message
        super().__init__(self.message)

# Raise the custom exception
def set_age(age):
    if age < 0:
        raise NegativeAgeError(age)
    return f"Age is set to {age}"

# Handling the custom exception
try:
    set_age(-10)
except NegativeAgeError as e:
    print(f"Error: {e.message} Age provided: {e.age}")
```

Key Points:

- Custom exceptions should inherit from Exception or one of its subclasses.

- Use __init__() to initialize custom attributes if needed.

- Custom exceptions improve code readability and provide clearer error handling.

What Are Common Python Exceptions (e.g., ValueError, KeyError, TypeError)?

Python has several built-in exceptions that cover a wide range of common errors. Here are some of the most frequently encountered:

1. **ValueError**

   Raised when a function receives an argument of the right type but an inappropriate value.

   ```
   int("abc")   # ValueError: invalid literal for int() with base 10
   ```

2. **KeyError**

   Raised when attempting to access a dictionary key that does not exist.

   ```
   my_dict = {"name": "Alice"}
   print(my_dict["age"])   # KeyError: 'age'
   ```

3. **TypeError**

   Raised when an operation or function is applied to an object of inappropriate type.

   ```
   result = 5 + "five"   # TypeError: unsupported operand type(s) for
   +: 'int' and 'str'
   ```

4. **IndexError**

   Raised when trying to access an element outside the valid range of a list or sequence.

   ```
   my_list = [1, 2, 3]
   print(my_list[5])   # IndexError: list index out of range
   ```

5. **ZeroDivisionError**

   Raised when attempting to divide by zero.

   ```
   result = 10 / 0   # ZeroDivisionError: division by zero
   ```

6. **FileNotFoundError**

   Raised when trying to open a file that does not exist.

   ```
   with open("nonexistent_file.txt") as file:
       content = file.read()   # FileNotFoundError: [Errno 2] No such
   file or directory
   ```

7. **AttributeError**

   Raised when an invalid attribute is accessed for an object.

```
my_string = "Hello"
my_string.append("!")  # AttributeError: 'str' object has no
attribute 'append'
```

8. **ImportError**

    Raised when an import statement fails to find the module or object being imported.

    ```
    import nonexistent_module  # ImportError: No module named
    'nonexistent_module'
    ```

Summary Table of Common Exceptions:

Exception	Description
ValueError	Wrong value for a valid type
KeyError	Accessing a non-existent dictionary key
TypeError	Inappropriate type for an operation
IndexError	Index out of range for a list or sequence
ZeroDivisionError	Division by zero
FileNotFoundError	File does not exist
AttributeError	Invalid attribute access
ImportError	Module or object not found during import

1.6 File Handling

How Do You Open and Read Files in Python Using the open() Function?

In Python, the open() function is used to work with files. It allows you to open a file and returns a file object that can be used to read, write, or manipulate the file's contents.

41

Syntax of open():

```
file_object = open('filename', 'mode')
```

- **filename**: The name or path of the file you want to open.

- **mode**: A string specifying the mode in which to open the file (e.g., read, write).

Basic Example:

```
# Opening a file in read mode
file = open('example.txt', 'r')

# Reading the file's content
content = file.read()
print(content)

# Always close the file after use
file.close()
```

Key Points:

- Always close the file using file.close() after you finish working with it.

- If the file doesn't exist when opening in read mode, Python raises a FileNotFoundError.

What Are the Modes for Opening Files in Python ('r', 'w', 'a', 'b')?

Python's open() function supports several modes for file handling, each determining how the file is accessed:

Mode	Description
'r'	Read mode (default). Opens the file for reading. File must exist.
'w'	Write mode. Opens the file for writing. If the file exists, it truncates (overwrites) it. If it doesn't exist, it creates a new file.

'a'	Append mode. Opens the file for writing and appends new data at the end. Creates the file if it doesn't exist.
'b'	Binary mode. Used with other modes ('rb', 'wb', 'ab') to read/write binary files like images.
'+'	Read and write mode. Can be combined with other modes (e.g., 'r+', 'w+').

Examples:

```python
# Open a file in binary read mode
file = open('image.jpg', 'rb')

# Open a file in append mode
file = open('log.txt', 'a')
```

How Do You Use read(), readline(), and readlines() to Read File Content?

Python provides several methods to read file content, each serving a specific purpose:

- **read() Method**

  Reads the entire content of the file as a single string. It's suitable for small files.

  ```python
  with open('example.txt', 'r') as file:
      content = file.read()
      print(content)
  ```

- **readline() Method**

  Reads one line from the file at a time. Useful for processing files line-by-line.

  ```python
  with open('example.txt', 'r') as file:
      line = file.readline()
      while line:
          print(line.strip())  # Remove the newline character
          line = file.readline()
  ```

43

- readlines() **Method**

  Reads all lines of the file into a list where each line is an element.

  ```python
  with open('example.txt', 'r') as file:
      lines = file.readlines()
      for line in lines:
          print(line.strip())
  ```

Comparison:

- read(): Reads the entire file as a string.

- readline(): Reads the file line-by-line.

- readlines(): Reads all lines into a list.

How Do You Write Data to Files in Python?

To write data to files in Python, use write() or writelines() methods with the file opened in 'w', 'a', or 'x' mode.

write() **Method**

Writes a string to the file. Use 'w' mode to overwrite the file or 'a' mode to append.

```python
# Writing to a file
with open('output.txt', 'w') as file:
    file.write("Hello, World!\n")
    file.write("This is a new line.")
```

writelines() **Method**

Writes a list of strings to the file. Each item in the list is written sequentially.

```python
# Writing multiple lines to a file
lines = ["First line\n", "Second line\n", "Third line\n"]
with open('output.txt', 'a') as file:
    file.writelines(lines)
```

44

Modes for Writing:

- **'w'**: Overwrites the file.

- **'a'**: Appends to the file.

- **'x'**: Creates a new file and writes to it (raises FileExistsError if the file already exists).

How Do You Handle File Exceptions and Errors (e.g., FileNotFoundError)?

To handle file-related errors gracefully, use try-except blocks. This ensures your program can manage common file errors without crashing.

Example Handling FileNotFoundError:

```
try:
    with open('nonexistent_file.txt', 'r') as file:
        content = file.read()
except FileNotFoundError:
    print("Error: The file does not exist.")
```

Handling Other File Errors:

You can handle multiple exceptions in one block or use a generic Exception to catch all file-related errors.

```
try:
    with open('data.txt', 'r') as file:
        content = file.read()
except FileNotFoundError:
    print("Error: File not found.")
except PermissionError:
    print("Error: You don't have permission to read this file.")
except Exception as e:
    print(f"An unexpected error occurred: {e}")
```

Best Practices:

- Use specific exceptions like FileNotFoundError or PermissionError to handle known scenarios.

- Use a finally block if you need to ensure resources are closed, but in file handling, it's often better to use the with statement.

45

What Is the Purpose of the with Statement When Working With Files?

The with statement in Python is used for resource management and ensures that files are properly closed after use, even if an error occurs. It is often called a **context manager**.

Benefits of Using with:

1. **Automatic Resource Management**: No need to explicitly call file.close().

2. **Cleaner Code**: Reduces boilerplate code.

3. **Error Safety**: Ensures that the file is closed even if an error occurs during file operations.

Syntax Example:

```python
# Using with statement to open a file
with open('example.txt', 'r') as file:
    content = file.read()
    print(content)
# No need to call file.close(); it's handled automatically.
```

How Do You Use os and shutil for File System Operations (e.g., Moving, Copying Files)?

Python's built-in os and shutil modules provide functions for interacting with the file system. They allow you to move, copy, delete, and manipulate files and directories.

Using os for Basic File Operations

- **Renaming a File:**

```python
import os

# Renaming a file
os.rename('old_name.txt', 'new_name.txt')
```

- **Removing a File:**

```python
# Deleting a file
os.remove('file_to_delete.txt')
```

- **Creating and Removing Directories:**

```python
# Creating a directory
os.mkdir('new_directory')

# Removing an empty directory
os.rmdir('empty_directory')
```

Using shutil for Advanced File Operations

- **Copying a File:**

```python
import shutil

# Copying a file
shutil.copy('source_file.txt', 'destination_file.txt')
```

- **Moving a File:**

```python
# Moving a file
shutil.move('file_to_move.txt', 'new_location/file_to_move.txt')
```

- **Deleting a Directory and Its Contents:**

```python
# Removing a directory and all its contents
shutil.rmtree('directory_to_remove')
```

Key Differences:

- os: Ideal for basic file operations like renaming, deleting, and directory manipulation.

- shutil: Better suited for more complex operations like copying files or directories and moving them.

1.7 Data Structures in Python

What Are the Differences Between Lists, Tuples, Sets, and Dictionaries?

Python includes several built-in data structures, each with its own features and uses:

1. **Lists**

    - **Definition**: An ordered, mutable collection that allows duplicate elements.

    - **Syntax**: my_list = [1, 2, 3, "apple"]

    - **Key Features**:

        ○ Supports indexing, slicing, and iteration.

        ○ Elements can be added, removed, or modified.

        ○ Commonly used for ordered data storage.

2. **Tuples**

    - **Definition**: An ordered, immutable collection that allows duplicate elements.

    - **Syntax**: my_tuple = (1, 2, 3, "apple")

    - **Key Features**:

        ○ Similar to lists, but cannot be modified after creation.

        ○ Often used for fixed collections of data (e.g., coordinates, configurations).

        ○ More memory-efficient compared to lists.

3. **Sets**

    - **Definition**: An unordered, mutable collection with no duplicate elements.

    - **Syntax**: my_set = {1, 2, 3, "apple"}

    - **Key Features**:

        ○ Useful for membership testing (in operator).

        ○ Supports mathematical set operations like union, intersection, and difference.

        ○ Cannot be indexed or sliced since it's unordered.

4. **Dictionaries**

    - **Definition**: An unordered collection of key-value pairs.

    - **Syntax**: my_dict = {"name": "Alice", "age": 25}

- **Key Features**:

  - Keys are unique and immutable; values can be any type.

  - Provides fast lookups, additions, and deletions based on keys.

  - Ideal for scenarios where data needs to be accessed by a unique identifier.

Comparison Table:

Data Structure	Order	Mutable	Allows Duplicates	Usage
List	Yes	Yes	Yes	General-purpose, ordered data
Tuple	Yes	No	Yes	Fixed data, configuration
Set	No	Yes	No	Unique elements, set operations
Dictionary	No	Yes (values)	Keys: No, Values: Yes	Key-value pairs, fast lookups

How Do You Use List and Dictionary Comprehensions to Create Complex Structures?

List Comprehension

List comprehensions provide a concise way to create lists using an expression inside square brackets.

```python
# Basic List Comprehension
squares = [x**2 for x in range(10)]
# Output: [0, 1, 4, 9, 16, 25, 36, 49, 64, 81]

# List Comprehension with Condition
even_squares = [x**2 for x in range(10) if x % 2 == 0]
# Output: [0, 4, 16, 36, 64]

# Nested List Comprehension
matrix = [[j for j in range(3)] for i in range(3)]
# Output: [[0, 1, 2], [0, 1, 2], [0, 1, 2]]
```

Dictionary Comprehension

Dictionary comprehensions allow you to create dictionaries using an expression inside curly braces.

```
# Basic Dictionary Comprehension
squares_dict = {x: x**2 for x in range(5)}
# Output: {0: 0, 1: 1, 2: 4, 3: 9, 4: 16}

# Dictionary Comprehension with Condition
odd_squares = {x: x**2 for x in range(10) if x % 2 != 0}
# Output: {1: 1, 3: 9, 5: 25, 7: 49, 9: 81}

# Inverting a dictionary
original = {"a": 1, "b": 2, "c": 3}
inverted = {v: k for k, v in original.items()}
# Output: {1: 'a', 2: 'b', 3: 'c'}
```

How Do You Sort Lists and Dictionaries in Python?

Sorting Lists

Python's sort() method and sorted() function allow you to sort lists.

- **sort() Method**: Sorts the list in place (modifies the original list).

- **sorted() Function**: Returns a new sorted list without modifying the original.

```
# In-place sorting
numbers = [5, 2, 9, 1]
numbers.sort()
# Output: [1, 2, 5, 9]

# Sorting with a custom key
words = ["banana", "apple", "cherry"]
words.sort(key=len)   # Sort by length of words
# Output: ['apple', 'banana', 'cherry']

# Using sorted() to create a sorted copy
numbers = [3, 6, 1, 4]
sorted_numbers = sorted(numbers, reverse=True)
# Output: [6, 4, 3, 1]
```

Sorting Dictionaries

Dictionaries are unordered, but you can sort them by keys or values.

```python
# Sorting a dictionary by keys
my_dict = {"b": 2, "a": 1, "c": 3}
sorted_by_keys = dict(sorted(my_dict.items()))
# Output: {'a': 1, 'b': 2, 'c': 3}
# Sorting a dictionary by values
sorted_by_values = dict(sorted(my_dict.items(), key=lambda item:
item[1]))
# Output: {'a': 1, 'b': 2, 'c': 3}
```

What Is the Difference Between Mutable and Immutable Types in Python?

Mutable Types

- Objects that can be changed after creation.

- Examples: **Lists**, **Dictionaries**, **Sets**.

Immutable Types

- Objects that cannot be changed after creation.

- Examples: **Tuples**, **Strings**, **Integers**, **Floats**.

Why Does It Matter?

1. **Performance**: Immutable objects are faster to access since their content does not change.

2. **Hashing**: Immutable objects can be used as dictionary keys or set elements, while mutable objects cannot.

3. **Safety**: Immutability can prevent unintended changes, making the code more reliable.

Example:

```python
# Mutable example
my_list = [1, 2, 3]
my_list[0] = 4  # Modifying an element (allowed)
# Immutable example
my_tuple = (1, 2, 3)
# my_tuple[0] = 4  # Raises a TypeError
```

How Do You Implement a Stack and a Queue Using Python's Built-In Data Structures?

Stack Implementation Using a List

A stack follows Last-In-First-Out (LIFO) order. You can use Python's list with append() and pop() methods.

```python
# Stack implementation
stack = []

# Push elements onto the stack
stack.append(1)
stack.append(2)
stack.append(3)

# Pop elements from the stack
top = stack.pop()   # Output: 3
```

Queue Implementation Using a List

A queue follows First-In-First-Out (FIFO) order. You can use append() and pop(0) methods, though it's not the most efficient way.

```python
# Queue implementation
queue = []

# Enqueue elements
queue.append('a')
queue.append('b')
queue.append('c')

# Dequeue elements
first = queue.pop(0)   # Output: 'a'
```

Efficient Queue Using collections.deque

collections.deque is a double-ended queue that supports fast append and pop operations from both ends.

```
from collections import deque

# Queue using deque
queue = deque()

# Enqueue
queue.append('x')
queue.append('y')

# Dequeue
first = queue.popleft()   # Output: 'x'
```

How Do You Use Python's Built-In collections Module (e.g., Counter, deque)?

The collections module provides specialized data structures like Counter, deque, defaultdict, and namedtuple.

1. **Counter**

   A subclass of dict for counting hashable objects.

   ```
   from collections import Counter

   # Counting elements
   fruits = ['apple', 'banana', 'apple', 'orange', 'banana', 'apple']
   count = Counter(fruits)
   # Output: Counter({'apple': 3, 'banana': 2, 'orange': 1})
   ```

2. **deque**

   A double-ended queue that allows fast appends and pops.

   ```
   from collections import deque

   # Using deque for efficient queues
   dq = deque([1, 2, 3])
   dq.appendleft(0)   # Adds to the front
   dq.append(4)       # Adds to the end
   dq.pop()           # Removes from the end
   ```

3. defaultdict

A dictionary that returns a default value if a key does not exist.

```python
from collections import defaultdict

# Using defaultdict
dd = defaultdict(int)
dd['a'] += 1  # If 'a' doesn't exist, it starts with 0 and then
increments
# Output: {'a': 1}
```

4. namedtuple

A factory function for creating tuple subclasses with named fields.

```python
from collections import namedtuple

# Creating a namedtuple
Point = namedtuple('Point', ['x', 'y'])
p = Point(10, 20)
# Accessing fields
print(p.x)  # Output: 10
```

How Do You Implement a Binary Search on a Sorted List?

Binary search is an efficient algorithm for finding an item in a sorted list. It works by repeatedly dividing the search interval in half.

Binary Search Algorithm:

1. Check the middle element of the list.

2. If it matches the target, return its index.

3. If the target is smaller, search the left half; if larger, search the right half.

4. Repeat until the target is found or the list is empty.

Implementation Example:

```python
def binary_search(arr, target):
    """Perform binary search on a sorted list."""
```

```
    left, right = 0, len(arr) - 1

    while left <= right:
        mid = (left + right) // 2
        if arr[mid] == target:
            return mid   # Target found
        elif arr[mid] < target:
            left = mid + 1   # Search right half
        else:
            right = mid - 1   # Search left half

    return -1   # Target not found

# Using the binary search function
numbers = [1, 3, 5, 7, 9, 11, 13]
index = binary_search(numbers, 7)   # Output: 3 (index of the target)
```

Time Complexity:

- **Binary Search**: $O(\log n)$ (very efficient for large sorted lists).

- **Linear Search**: $O(n)$ (less efficient for large lists).

1.8 Object-Oriented Programming (OOP) Basics

What Are Classes and Objects in Python, and How Are They Defined?

In Python, **classes** are blueprints for creating objects (instances). An **object** is an instance of a class, representing a specific realization of that class with its own data and behavior.

Defining a Class

Classes in Python are defined using the class keyword, followed by the class name (using CamelCase by convention).

```
# Defining a simple class
class Person:
    # Class constructor (initializer)
```

```
    def __init__(self, name, age):
        self.name = name   # Attribute
        self.age = age     # Attribute
    # Method to display information
    def introduce(self):
        print(f"My name is {self.name} and I am {self.age} years old.")
# Creating an object (instance) of the class
person1 = Person("Alice", 30)
person1.introduce()   # Output: My name is Alice and I am 30 years old.
```

Key Concepts:

- **Class**: A blueprint that defines a type with attributes and methods.

- **Object**: An instance of a class with its own set of data.

- **Attributes**: Variables that belong to an object (e.g., name, age).

- **Methods**: Functions that belong to a class and define behavior.

What Is the self Parameter, and Why Is It Required in Class Methods?

The self parameter is a reference to the current instance of the class. It allows access to the instance's attributes and methods. self is required in all instance methods to access data that belongs to the object.

Key Points:

1. self is automatically passed by Python when a method is called on an object.

2. It's a convention to name the first parameter self, but you can technically use any name (though it's not recommended).

Example:

```
class Animal:
    def __init__(self, species):
        self.species = species   # Using self to assign an attribute
    def speak(self):
        print(f"The {self.species} makes a sound.")
# Creating an instance and accessing attributes via self
dog = Animal("Dog")
dog.speak()   # Output: The Dog makes a sound.
```

What Is the Difference Between a Class Method and an Instance Method?

Python supports different types of methods in a class:

Instance Method

- Belongs to an instance of a class.

- Requires the self parameter.

- Can access or modify the instance's data.

```python
class Car:
    def __init__(self, model):
        self.model = model  # Instance attribute

    def display_model(self):
        return f"The car model is {self.model}."  # Instance method
```

Class Method

- Belongs to the class itself, not any particular instance.

- Uses the @classmethod decorator.

- The first parameter is cls, which refers to the class.

- Commonly used for factory methods or operations that apply to the class as a whole.

```python
class Car:
    count = 0  # Class attribute

    def __init__(self, model):
        self.model = model
        Car.count += 1

    @classmethod
    def total_cars(cls):
        return f"Total cars created: {cls.count}"  # Class method
```

Key Differences:

- **Instance Methods**: Operate on an instance; require self.

- **Class Methods**: Operate on the class; require cls

How Do You Implement Inheritance in Python?

Inheritance is a fundamental concept in OOP that allows one class to inherit attributes and methods from another class, promoting code reuse.

Basic Inheritance Example:

```python
# Base (Parent) class
class Animal:
    def __init__(self, name):
        self.name = name

    def eat(self):
        print(f"{self.name} is eating.")

# Derived (Child) class inheriting from Animal
class Dog(Animal):
    def bark(self):
        print(f"{self.name} is barking.")

# Creating an instance of the derived class
dog = Dog("Buddy")
dog.eat()    # Inherited method from Animal
dog.bark()   # Method from Dog
```

Key Concepts:

- **Base Class (Parent)**: The class being inherited from.

- **Derived Class (Child)**: The class that inherits from the base class.

- Methods and attributes of the parent class are accessible in the child class.

What Are Python's Built-In Dunder Methods (e.g., __init__, __str__, __repr__)?

Dunder (Double Underscore) Methods, also known as **magic methods**, are special methods with double underscores before and after their names. These methods enable Python's built-in operations and behaviors, making objects behave like built-in types.

Common Dunder Methods:

1. __init__:

   The initializer or constructor. Called when an object is created.

   ```python
   def __init__(self, name, age):
       self.name = name
       self.age = age
   ```

2. __str__:

   Defines the human-readable string representation of an object. Called by print() or str().

   ```python
   def __str__(self):
       return f"Person(name={self.name}, age={self.age})"
   ```

3. __repr__:

   Defines the official string representation of an object, often used for debugging. Called by repr().

   ```python
   def __repr__(self):
       return f"Person('{self.name}', {self.age})"
   ```

Example Using Dunder Methods:

```python
class Person:
    def __init__(self, name, age):
        self.name = name
        self.age = age

    def __str__(self):
        return f"{self.name}, {self.age} years old"

    def __repr__(self):
        return f"Person('{self.name}', {self.age})"

# Creating an object
p = Person("Alice", 30)
print(p)         # Output: Alice, 30 years old (uses __str__)
print(repr(p))   # Output: Person('Alice', 30) (uses __repr__)
```

What Is Encapsulation, and How Do You Enforce It Using Private Members?

Encapsulation is the concept of restricting direct access to some of an object's components and protecting the internal state from unintended modifications. It is achieved through **private** and **protected** members.

Access Modifiers in Python:

1. **Public**: Accessible from anywhere. Default visibility (e.g., self.name).

2. **Protected**: Should not be accessed outside the class (convention only). Use a single underscore (e.g., self._name).

3. **Private**: Not accessible outside the class. Use double underscores (e.g., self.__name).

Example of Encapsulation:

```python
class Account:
    def __init__(self, owner, balance):
        self.owner = owner          # Public attribute
        self._balance = balance     # Protected attribute
        self.__pin = "1234"         # Private attribute

    def deposit(self, amount):
        if amount > 0:
            self._balance += amount
            print(f"Deposited {amount}. New balance: {self._balance}")

    def __verify_pin(self, pin):    # Private method
        return pin == self.__pin

# Accessing members
account = Account("Alice", 1000)
print(account.owner)        # Public: OK
print(account._balance)     # Protected: OK (but should be avoided)
# print(account.__pin)      # Error: AttributeError (private)
```

Why Use Encapsulation?

- **Data Protection**: Prevents unintended access or modification.

- **Code Maintenance**: Hides implementation details, making the code easier to modify without affecting external code.

What Is the Role of super() in Python Inheritance?

The super() function is used to call a method from the parent class. It is often used to extend or override the behavior of the parent class in the child class.

Key Use Cases:

1. Call the parent's __init__ method to initialize inherited attributes.

2. Extend or modify methods in the child class while still accessing the parent's functionality.

Example Using super():

```python
class Animal:
    def __init__(self, name):
        self.name = name

    def speak(self):
        return "Some generic sound"

# Child class extending Animal
class Dog(Animal):
    def __init__(self, name, breed):
        super().__init__(name)  # Calling the parent's __init__
        self.breed = breed

    def speak(self):
        return f"{self.name} says Woof!"

# Creating instances
dog = Dog("Buddy", "Golden Retriever")
print(dog.speak())  # Output: Buddy says Woof!
```

Advantages of super():

- **Simplifies Code**: Avoids directly referencing the parent class, making it easier to maintain and extend.

- **Multiple Inheritance**: Facilitates calling methods from multiple parent classes in complex inheritance scenarios.

1.9 Modules and Packages

What Is a Module in Python, and How Do You Import It?

A **module** in Python is a file containing Python code (functions, classes, variables) that you can import and use in other Python programs. It helps organize code into logical components, making it reusable and manageable.

Creating and Importing a Module:

1. Create a file named mymodule.py with the following code:

```python
# mymodule.py
def greet(name):
    return f"Hello, {name}!"
```

2. Import and use the module in another file:

```python
# main.py
import mymodule

message = mymodule.greet("Alice")
print(message)  # Output: Hello, Alice!
```

Key Points:

- The file name (without .py) is the module name.

- Use import module_name to import the entire module.

- Use module_name.function_name() to access functions from the module.

What Is the Difference Between import module and from module import?

There are different ways to import modules in Python, each serving a specific purpose:

import module:

- Imports the entire module.

- Access functions, classes, and variables using the module's name as a prefix.

- **Example**:

```
import math
print(math.sqrt(16))   # Output: 4.0
```

from module import:

- Imports specific elements from a module.

- Access imported functions, classes, or variables directly without the module name.

- **Example**:

```
from math import sqrt
print(sqrt(16))   # Output: 4.0
```

Differences:

- **import module**: Keeps the namespace organized, but can be verbose.

- **from module import**: Provides direct access to elements but can lead to name conflicts if not used carefully.

How Do You Create Your Own Python Package?

A **package** is a collection of modules grouped together in a directory with an __init__.py file (to indicate it's a package). This allows you to organize related modules in a hierarchical structure.

Steps to Create a Package:

1. **Create a directory** with the package name:

```
mypackage/
```

2. **Add an __init__.py file** inside the directory (can be empty):

```
mypackage/
    __init__.py
    module1.py
    module2.py
```

3. **Create modules** inside the package:

```
# module1.py
def greet():
    return "Hello from Module 1!"


# module2.py
def farewell():
    return "Goodbye from Module 2!"
```

4. **Import and use the package**:

```
# main.py
from mypackage import module1, module2

print(module1.greet())    # Output: Hello from Module 1!
print(module2.farewell()) # Output: Goodbye from Module 2!
```

Key Points:

- The __init__.py file can be empty or used to execute initialization code when the package is imported.

- Modules inside the package can be imported using dot notation (from package.module import function).

How Do You Organize Code Using Packages and Sub-Packages in Python?

To organize code into packages and sub-packages, follow a hierarchical directory structure. Sub-packages are simply directories within packages that contain their own __init__.py file.

Example Directory Structure:

```
project/
    main.py
    mypackage/
        __init__.py
        module1.py
        subpackage/
            __init__.py
            submodule.py
```

64

Example of Using Sub-Packages:

```python
# mypackage/module1.py
def greet():
    return "Hello from Module 1!"

# mypackage/subpackage/submodule.py
def info():
    return "This is a sub-module."

# main.py
from mypackage import module1
from mypackage.subpackage import submodule
print(module1.greet())      # Output: Hello from Module 1!
print(submodule.info())     # Output: This is a sub-module.
```

Tips:

- Keep related functionality together in the same module or sub-package.

- Use clear and descriptive names for packages, sub-packages, and modules.

How Do You Use pip for Installing and Managing Python Libraries?

pip is Python's package manager used to install, upgrade, and manage third-party Python libraries.

Common pip Commands:

1. **Installing a Package**:

   ```
   pip install requests
   ```

2. **Upgrading a Package**:

   ```
   pip install --upgrade requests
   ```

3. **Uninstalling a Package**:

   ```
   pip uninstall requests
   ```

4. **Listing Installed Packages**:

```
pip list
```

5. **Saving Installed Packages to** requirements.txt:

```
pip freeze > requirements.txt
```

6. **Installing Packages from** requirements.txt:

```
pip install -r requirements.txt
```

Best Practices:

- Use virtual environments to manage dependencies for individual projects.

- Keep a requirements.txt file to list all required packages with specific versions.

What Are the Differences Between Built-In and Third-Party Libraries in Python?

Python has a rich ecosystem of both built-in and third-party libraries. Here's a comparison:

Built-In Libraries:

- Come with Python's standard library (no need to install separately).

- Provide core functionalities like file handling (os), math operations (math), data structures (collections), and network interactions (socket).

- Always available and reliable, as they are maintained by the Python core team.

- **Example**:

```
import os
files = os.listdir('.')  # List files in the current directory
```

Third-Party Libraries:

- Developed and maintained by the community or companies.

- Need to be installed using a package manager like pip.

- Extend Python's capabilities, offering advanced functionality not covered by the standard library.

- **Examples**: requests (HTTP library), NumPy (numerical computing), pandas (data analysis).

- **Example**:

```
import requests
response = requests.get('https://api.example.com/data')
print(response.json())
```

Key Differences:

- **Built-In**: Reliable, no installation required, part of the standard library.

- **Third-Party**: More specialized, require installation, may vary in quality and support.

How Do You Use Popular Libraries Like requests, NumPy, and pandas?

1. **requests Library**

   The requests library is a popular third-party module for making HTTP requests. It simplifies interacting with web APIs.

   Installation:

   ```
   pip install requests
   ```

   Usage Example:

   ```
   import requests

   response =
   requests.get('https://jsonplaceholder.typicode.com/posts/1')
   data = response.json()
   print(data['title'])   # Output: Title of the post
   ```

2. **NumPy Library**

   NumPy is a powerful library for numerical computing, offering support for arrays, matrices, and advanced mathematical operations.

   Installation:

   ```
   pip install numpy
   ```

Usage Example:

```python
import numpy as np

# Creating a NumPy array
arr = np.array([1, 2, 3, 4, 5])

# Basic operations
print(arr.mean())    # Output: 3.0
print(arr * 2)       # Output: [2 4 6 8 10]
```

3. **pandas Library**

   pandas is a widely-used data analysis library that provides data structures like DataFrame for handling tabular data.

   Installation:

   ```
   pip install pandas
   ```

   Usage Example:

   ```python
   import pandas as pd

   # Creating a DataFrame from a dictionary
   data = {'Name': ['Alice', 'Bob', 'Charlie'],
           'Age': [25, 30, 35]}
   df = pd.DataFrame(data)

   # Accessing data
   print(df.head())   # Display the first few rows
   print(df['Age'].mean())   # Calculate the average age
   ```

Comparison of Popular Libraries:

Library	Purpose	Key Features
requests	HTTP requests and web API interactions	Simplified API, handles JSON, sessions, authentication
NumPy	Numerical computing and mathematical operations	Arrays, matrices, linear algebra, random numbers

pandas	Data manipulation and analysis	DataFrames, data cleaning, group operations, statistics

1.10 Introduction to Unit Testing

What Is Unit Testing, and Why Is It Important for Python Development?

Unit Testing:

Unit testing is a software testing technique where individual units or components of a software application are tested in isolation to verify that they work as expected. In Python, these units are typically functions, methods, or classes.

Why Is It Important?

1. **Catch Errors Early**: Unit tests help identify bugs and logic errors early in the development process, reducing the cost of fixing issues.

2. **Improve Code Quality**: By writing tests, developers are encouraged to write cleaner and more modular code.

3. **Ensure Code Stability**: Automated unit tests allow for safer refactoring, as they can quickly verify that changes haven't broken existing functionality.

4. **Documentation**: Tests serve as a form of documentation by demonstrating how code is supposed to be used and what the expected outcomes are.

5. **Faster Development**: A robust suite of unit tests speeds up development by catching errors automatically, leading to faster iterations and feedback.

How Do You Write Basic Unit Tests Using the unittest Module?

Python's built-in unittest module is the standard way to write and run unit tests. It follows the xUnit style of testing (similar to JUnit for Java or NUnit for .NET).

Basic Example:

1. **Creating a Function to Test:**

```
# math_functions.py
```

69

```python
def add(x, y):
    return x + y

def subtract(x, y):
    return x - y
```

2. **Writing Unit Tests**:

```python
# test_math_functions.py
import unittest
from math_functions import add, subtract

class TestMathFunctions(unittest.TestCase):
    # Test cases for the add function
    def test_add(self):
        self.assertEqual(add(3, 5), 8)
        self.assertEqual(add(-1, 1), 0)
        self.assertEqual(add(0, 0), 0)

    # Test cases for the subtract function
    def test_subtract(self):
        self.assertEqual(subtract(10, 5), 5)
        self.assertEqual(subtract(0, 0), 0)
        self.assertEqual(subtract(5, 10), -5)

# Running the tests
if __name__ == '__main__':
    unittest.main()
```

Key Concepts:

- unittest.TestCase: A class from which all test cases should inherit.

- **Test Method**: Methods inside the TestCase class that start with test_. These methods are automatically discovered and run by the test runner.

How Do You Use assert Statements in Python Tests?

In unit tests, assertions are used to verify that the output of a function matches the expected result. If the assertion fails, the test will fail.

Common Assertion Methods:

Assertion	Description
assertEqual(a, b)	Checks if a is equal to b.
assertNotEqual(a, b)	Checks if a is not equal to b.
assertTrue(x)	Checks if x is True.
assertFalse(x)	Checks if x is False.
assertIn(a, b)	Checks if a is in b.
assertIsNone(x)	Checks if x is None.
assertRaises(exception)	Checks if an exception is raised.

Example:

```python
class TestAssertions(unittest.TestCase):
    def test_assertions(self):
        self.assertEqual(5 + 5, 10)
        self.assertTrue(3 < 5)
        self.assertFalse(5 < 3)
        self.assertIn("h", "hello")
        self.assertIsNone(None)
        with self.assertRaises(ZeroDivisionError):
            1 / 0
```

What Is the setUp() and tearDown() Methods in unittest?

The setUp() and tearDown() methods are special methods in unittest used to prepare and clean up the test environment. They are executed before and after each test method, respectively.

Purpose:

- setUp(): Initializes resources (e.g., database connections, mock data) required for tests.

- tearDown(): Cleans up resources, ensuring a fresh environment for each test.

Example:

```
class TestSetupTeardown(unittest.TestCase):
    def setUp(self):
        # Setup code before each test
        self.list = [1, 2, 3]

    def tearDown(self):
        # Cleanup code after each test
        self.list = None

    def test_list_length(self):
        self.assertEqual(len(self.list), 3)

    def test_list_content(self):
        self.assertIn(2, self.list)
```

Alternative: setUpClass() **and** tearDownClass()**:**

- Use @classmethod decorator.

- Executed once before and after all tests in the class.

- Ideal for setting up expensive resources.

What Are the Benefits of Using the pytest Framework for Testing?

While unittest is the built-in testing framework, **pytest** is a popular third-party framework that offers more advanced features, simpler syntax, and better error reporting.

Benefits of pytest:

1. **Less Boilerplate**: No need to inherit from unittest.TestCase. Use simple functions for tests.

2. **Powerful Assertions**: Built-in assertion introspection provides detailed error messages.

3. **Plugins**: A wide range of plugins (e.g., for test coverage, benchmarking) is available.

4. **Fixtures**: Use fixtures for managing complex setup and teardown scenarios.

5. **Parameterization**: Allows running the same test with multiple sets of data using @pytest.mark.parametrize.

Example Using pytest:

1. **Test File (test_math_functions.py)**:

```python
# test_math_functions.py
from math_functions import add, subtract


def test_add():
    assert add(3, 5) == 8
    assert add(-1, 1) == 0


def test_subtract():
    assert subtract(10, 5) == 5
    assert subtract(5, 10) == -5
```

2. **Running Tests**:

```
pytest test_math_functions.py
```

How Do You Perform Test-Driven Development (TDD) in Python?

Test-Driven Development (TDD) is a software development approach where tests are written before the code. The process involves:

1. **Write a Test**: Create a test that defines the desired functionality.

2. **Run the Test**: It should fail initially, indicating the functionality is not yet implemented.

3. **Write the Code**: Implement the functionality to make the test pass.

4. **Run the Test Again**: Ensure the test passes.

5. **Refactor**: Improve the code while keeping tests passing.

Example of TDD:

1. **Step 1 - Write a Test**:

```python
# test_calculator.py
import unittest
from calculator import Calculator


class TestCalculator(unittest.TestCase):
```

```
    def test_add(self):
        calc = Calculator()
        self.assertEqual(calc.add(2, 3), 5)

 if __name__ == '__main__':
        unittest.main()
```

2. **Step 2 - Run the Test**:

    The test fails because the Calculator class does not exist yet.

3. **Step 3 - Write the Code**:

```
    # calculator.py
 class Calculator:
        def add(self, x, y):
            return x + y
```

4. **Step 4 - Run the Test Again**:

    The test should now pass.

5. **Step 5 - Refactor**:

    Improve code structure if needed while keeping the tests green.

How Do You Use Mocking for Testing Functions in Python?

Mocking is a technique used to simulate the behavior of complex objects or functions during testing. Python's unittest.mock module provides tools to replace parts of the system under test with mock objects.

Common Use Cases:

- Mocking database calls to avoid interacting with a real database.

- Simulating network requests.

- Replacing functions that have side effects (e.g., file operations).

Basic Mocking Example:

```
from unittest import TestCase
from unittest.mock import MagicMock
```

```python
# Function to be tested
def get_user_data(api_client, user_id):
    response = api_client.get(f"/users/{user_id}")
    return response.json()

class TestUserData(TestCase):
    def test_get_user_data(self):
        # Create a mock API client
        mock_client = MagicMock()
        mock_client.get.return_value.json.return_value = {"id": 1,
"name": "Alice"}

        # Call the function with the mock client
        result = get_user_data(mock_client, 1)
        # Assertions
        self.assertEqual(result, {"id": 1, "name": "Alice"})
        mock_client.get.assert_called_once_with("/users/1")
```

Key Tools for Mocking:

- **MagicMock**: A versatile mock object that can simulate any behavior.

- **patch**: A context manager or decorator that temporarily replaces a target with a mock object.

- **Mock**: A simpler version of MagicMock.

Using patch Example:

```python
from unittest import TestCase
from unittest.mock import patch

class TestFileOperations(TestCase):
    @patch('builtins.open')
    def test_open_file(self, mock_open):
        mock_open.return_value.read.return_value = "Mocked file content"
        # Test code using the mocked open
        with open('some_file.txt', 'r') as file:
            content = file.read()
        self.assertEqual(content, "Mocked file content")
        mock_open.assert_called_once_with('some_file.txt', 'r')
```

Section 2: Intermediate Questions

2.1 Advanced Data Structures and Algorithms

How Do You Implement Linked Lists in Python?

Linked List Overview:

A **linked list** is a linear data structure where elements are stored in nodes, and each node points to the next one in the sequence. Linked lists are beneficial when you need dynamic memory allocation or efficient insertion/deletion operations compared to arrays.

Node Definition:

```python
class Node:
    def __init__(self, data):
        self.data = data  # Stores the data
        self.next = None  # Points to the next node
```

Singly Linked List Implementation:

```python
class LinkedList:
    def __init__(self):
        self.head = None  # Initialize an empty list with head as None

    # Method to add a node at the beginning
    def insert_at_beginning(self, data):
        new_node = Node(data)
        new_node.next = self.head  # Point the new node to the old head
        self.head = new_node       # Update head to the new node

    # Method to add a node at the end
    def insert_at_end(self, data):
        new_node = Node(data)
        if not self.head:
            self.head = new_node
            return
        current = self.head
        while current.next:
            current = current.next
```

```
            current.next = new_node

        # Method to print the list
    def print_list(self):
        current = self.head
        while current:
            print(current.data, end=" -> ")
            current = current.next
        print("None")

# Example usage
ll = LinkedList()
ll.insert_at_beginning(10)
ll.insert_at_end(20)
ll.insert_at_end(30)
ll.print_list()  # Output: 10 -> 20 -> 30 -> None
```

Key Operations:

- **Insertion**: Adding a node at the beginning or end.

- **Deletion**: Removing a node by adjusting the next pointers.

- **Traversal**: Iterating through the nodes.

How Do You Build Stacks and Queues Using Python's Built-In Lists?

Stack Implementation Using Lists:

A **stack** is a LIFO (Last In, First Out) data structure. In Python, you can use a list with append() and pop() methods.

```
# Stack implementation using a list
stack = []
# Push elements onto the stack
stack.append(1)
stack.append(2)
stack.append(3)
# Pop elements from the stack
top = stack.pop()  # Output: 3
print(top)
```

Queue Implementation Using Lists:

A **queue** is a FIFO (First In, First Out) data structure. You can use append() for enqueue and pop(0) for dequeue, but it's not the most efficient method.

```
# Queue implementation using a list
queue = []

# Enqueue elements
queue.append('a')
queue.append('b')
queue.append('c')

# Dequeue elements
first = queue.pop(0)    # Output: 'a'
print(first)
```

Efficient Queue Using collections.deque:

For a more efficient queue, use the deque class from the collections module.

```
from collections import deque

# Queue using deque
queue = deque()

# Enqueue
queue.append('x')
queue.append('y')

# Dequeue
first = queue.popleft()    # Output: 'x'
```

How Do You Implement Binary Search Trees in Python?

Binary Search Tree (BST) Overview:

A **Binary Search Tree** is a binary tree where each node has at most two children, and the left child's value is less than the parent, while the right child's value is greater.

Node Definition:

```python
class TreeNode:
    def __init__(self, key):
        self.key = key
        self.left = None
        self.right = None
```

BST Implementation:

```python
class BinarySearchTree:
    def __init__(self):
        self.root = None

    # Method to insert a new node
    def insert(self, key):
        if self.root is None:
            self.root = TreeNode(key)
        else:
            self._insert_recursive(self.root, key)

    # Helper method for recursive insertion
    def _insert_recursive(self, node, key):
        if key < node.key:
            if node.left is None:
                node.left = TreeNode(key)
            else:
                self._insert_recursive(node.left, key)
        else:
            if node.right is None:
                node.right = TreeNode(key)
            else:
                self._insert_recursive(node.right, key)

    # Method to search for a value in the BST
    def search(self, key):
        return self._search_recursive(self.root, key)

    # Helper method for recursive search
    def _search_recursive(self, node, key):
```

```
        if node is None or node.key == key:
            return node
        if key < node.key:
            return self._search_recursive(node.left, key)
        return self._search_recursive(node.right, key)

# Example usage
bst = BinarySearchTree()
bst.insert(10)
bst.insert(5)
bst.insert(15)
result = bst.search(5)
print(result.key if result else "Not found")   # Output: 5
```

Key Operations:

- **Insertion**: Adds elements while maintaining BST properties.

- **Search**: Searches elements in $O(\log n)$ time if the tree is balanced.

- **Traversal**: Inorder traversal gives a sorted list of elements.

How Do You Implement Hash Maps Using Python Dictionaries?

Hash Map Overview:

A **Hash Map** is a data structure that maps keys to values using a hash function. In Python, the built-in dict type is a hash map.

Basic Hash Map Operations:

```
# Creating a dictionary
my_dict = {
    "name": "Alice",
    "age": 30,
    "job": "Engineer"
}

# Accessing values
print(my_dict["name"])   # Output: Alice

# Adding or updating values
```

```
my_dict["age"] = 31

# Removing a key-value pair
del my_dict["job"]

# Checking if a key exists
if "name" in my_dict:
    print("Key 'name' exists")
```

Key Points:

- **Insertion, Deletion, Lookup**: Average time complexity is $O(1)$ due to hashing.

- **Keys** must be immutable (e.g., strings, numbers, tuples).

- **Values** can be any data type.

What Is the Time Complexity of Basic Operations (e.g., Insertion, Deletion) on Lists, Sets, and Dictionaries?

Time Complexity Table:

Data Structure	Operation	Time Complexity	Explanation
List	Insertion (end)	$O(1)$	Appending to the end
	Insertion (middle)	$O(n)$	Shifting elements
	Deletion (end)	$O(1)$	Removing the last element
	Deletion (middle)	$O(n)$	Shifting elements
	Lookup by index	$O(1)$	Direct access
	Search by value	$O(n)$	Scanning the list
Set	Insertion	$O(1)$	Average-case

	Deletion	O(1)	Average-case
	Membership test	O(1)	Hash-based lookup
Dictionary	Insertion	O(1)	Average-case
	Deletion	O(1)	Average-case
	Lookup	O(1)	Average-case

Key Takeaways:

- **Lists** are ideal for ordered collections but can be inefficient for middle insertions or deletions.

- **Sets** and **Dictionaries** offer efficient membership testing, insertions, and deletions due to their hash-based implementation.

How Do You Optimize Sorting Algorithms in Python (e.g., QuickSort, MergeSort)?

QuickSort:

A **divide-and-conquer** algorithm that picks a pivot, partitions the array, and recursively sorts the partitions. It's efficient with an average-case complexity of O(n log n).

```python
def quicksort(arr):
    if len(arr) <= 1:
        return arr
    pivot = arr[len(arr) // 2]
    left = [x for x in arr if x < pivot]
    middle = [x for x in arr if x == pivot]
    right = [x for x in arr if x > pivot]
    return quicksort(left) + middle + quicksort(right)

# Example usage
numbers = [3, 6, 1, 8, 4, 5]
sorted_numbers = quicksort(numbers)
print(sorted_numbers)  # Output: [1, 3, 4, 5, 6, 8]
```

MergeSort:

A **stable, divide-and-conquer** algorithm that splits the array in half, sorts each half, and merges them. Has a consistent $O(n \log n)$ complexity.

```python
def merge_sort(arr):
    if len(arr) <= 1:
        return arr

    mid = len(arr) // 2
    left = merge_sort(arr[:mid])
    right = merge_sort(arr[mid:])

    return merge(left, right)

def merge(left, right):
    sorted_list = []
    i = j = 0
    while i < len(left) and j < len(right):
        if left[i] < right[j]:
            sorted_list.append(left[i])
            i += 1
        else:
            sorted_list.append(right[j])
            j += 1
    sorted_list.extend(left[i:])
    sorted_list.extend(right[j:])
    return sorted_list

# Example usage
numbers = [3, 6, 1, 8, 4, 5]
sorted_numbers = merge_sort(numbers)
print(sorted_numbers)  # Output: [1, 3, 4, 5, 6, 8]
```

Optimization Tips:

- Use **Timsort** (Python's default sorted() algorithm) for most practical use cases as it combines MergeSort and InsertionSort.

- Use **in-place sorting** for space efficiency when applicable.

How Do You Solve Common Algorithmic Problems Like Two-Sum, Fibonacci, and Palindrome Check?

1. **Two-Sum Problem**

   Given a list of numbers, find two numbers that add up to a specific target.

   ```python
   def two_sum(nums, target):
       lookup = {}
       for i, num in enumerate(nums):
           complement = target - num
           if complement in lookup:
               return [lookup[complement], i]
           lookup[num] = i

   # Example usage
   nums = [2, 7, 11, 15]
   target = 9
   result = two_sum(nums, target)  # Output: [0, 1] (nums[0] +
   nums[1] = 9)
   ```

2. **Fibonacci Sequence**

   Generate the nth Fibonacci number using a recursive and iterative approach.

   ```python
   # Recursive Fibonacci (inefficient)
   def fibonacci_recursive(n):
       if n <= 1:
           return n
       return fibonacci_recursive(n - 1) + fibonacci_recursive(n - 2)

   # Iterative Fibonacci (efficient)
   def fibonacci_iterative(n):
       a, b = 0, 1
       for _ in range(n):
           a, b = b, a + b
       return a

   # Example usage
   print(fibonacci_iterative(10))  # Output: 55
   ```

3. Palindrome Check

Check if a string is a palindrome (reads the same forward and backward).

```python
def is_palindrome(s):
    # Removing non-alphanumeric characters and converting to
Lowercase
    cleaned = ''.join(c.lower() for c in s if c.isalnum())
    return cleaned == cleaned[::-1]

# Example usage
print(is_palindrome("A man, a plan, a canal: Panama"))  # Output:
True
```

2.2 Advanced Object-Oriented Programming (OOP)

How Do You Implement Polymorphism in Python?

Polymorphism is an OOP concept that allows objects of different types to be treated as objects of a common super type. In Python, polymorphism is commonly achieved using methods and operator overloading.

Method Polymorphism Example:

```python
class Dog:
    def speak(self):
        return "Woof!"

class Cat:
    def speak(self):
        return "Meow!"

# Using polymorphism
def animal_speak(animal):
    return animal.speak()

dog = Dog()
cat = Cat()
```

```
print(animal_speak(dog))   # Output: Woof!
print(animal_speak(cat))   # Output: Meow!
```

Key Concepts:

- The animal_speak function can work with any object that has a speak method, demonstrating polymorphism.

- Python allows **duck typing**, meaning if an object "looks like a duck and quacks like a duck," it is treated like a duck.

What Are Abstract Classes and Interfaces, and How Do You Use abc Module?

Abstract Classes are classes that cannot be instantiated directly. They are designed to be subclasses and often contain one or more abstract methods (methods that must be implemented in child classes). In Python, the abc (Abstract Base Class) module allows you to create abstract classes and enforce interface-like behavior.

Using the abc Module:

1. **Import ABC and abstractmethod**:

```
from abc import ABC, abstractmethod
```

2. **Define an Abstract Class**:

```
class Animal(ABC):
    @abstractmethod
    def speak(self):
        pass
```

3. **Implement the Abstract Class**:

```
class Dog(Animal):
    def speak(self):
        return "Woof!"

class Cat(Animal):
    def speak(self):
        return "Meow!"
```

88

4. Instantiation Example:

```
# animal = Animal()  # Raises an error: Can't instantiate abstract
class
dog = Dog()
print(dog.speak())  # Output: Woof!
```

Key Points:

- **Abstract methods** must be overridden in subclasses.

- **Abstract classes** can have implemented methods, serving as a base for subclasses.

- **Interfaces** can be mimicked using abstract classes without any concrete implementation.

How Do You Implement Method Overloading and Overriding in Python?

Method Overloading:

Python does not support traditional method overloading (having multiple methods with the same name but different parameters). Instead, you can use default arguments or variable-length arguments (*args and **kwargs).

Method Overloading Example Using Default Arguments:

```
class MathOperations:
    def multiply(self, x, y=1):  # y is optional
        return x * y

math = MathOperations()
print(math.multiply(5))       # Output: 5
print(math.multiply(5, 2))    # Output: 10
```

Method Overriding:

Method overriding occurs when a subclass provides a specific implementation of a method that is already defined in its parent class.

Method Overriding Example:

```
class Parent:
    def greet(self):
        return "Hello from the Parent!"
```

```
class Child(Parent):
    def greet(self):
        return "Hello from the Child!"  # Overrides Parent's greet

# Example usage
parent = Parent()
child = Child()

print(parent.greet())  # Output: Hello from the Parent!
print(child.greet())   # Output: Hello from the Child!
```

Key Differences:

- **Overloading**: Achieved using default parameters; not true method overloading.

- **Overriding**: Inherited methods are replaced in the subclass.

What Is the Difference Between Static, Class, and Instance Methods?

Instance Methods:

- The most common type of method in Python.

- Require self as the first parameter.

- Operate on an instance of the class.

- Can access and modify instance attributes.

Class Methods:

- Use the @classmethod decorator.

- Require cls (the class itself) as the first parameter.

- Can modify class state that applies across all instances.

Static Methods:

- Use the @staticmethod decorator.

- Don't require self or cls.

- Cannot access or modify class/instance attributes.

- Behave like regular functions but reside within the class for organizational purposes.

Examples:

```python
class Example:
    class_variable = "Class Variable"

    def __init__(self, instance_variable):
        self.instance_variable = instance_variable

    # Instance Method
    def instance_method(self):
        return f"Instance: {self.instance_variable}"

    # Class Method
    @classmethod
    def class_method(cls):
        return f"Class: {cls.class_variable}"

    # Static Method
    @staticmethod
    def static_method():
        return "Static Method: Does not access class or instance data."

# Example usage
example = Example("Instance Data")
print(example.instance_method())   # Output: Instance: Instance Data
print(Example.class_method())      # Output: Class: Class Variable
print(Example.static_method())     # Output: Static Method: Does not
access class or instance data.
```

Key Takeaways:

- **Instance Methods** interact with specific instances.

- **Class Methods** interact with the class as a whole.

- **Static Methods** don't interact with instances or classes directly.

How Do You Use Property Decorators (@property) for Getter and Setter Methods?

The @property decorator is used to define methods that act like attributes, providing a Pythonic way to access and modify data while maintaining encapsulation.

Basic Example:

```python
class Circle:
    def __init__(self, radius):
        self._radius = radius  # Private variable

    # Getter
    @property
    def radius(self):
        return self._radius

    # Setter
    @radius.setter
    def radius(self, value):
        if value < 0:
            raise ValueError("Radius cannot be negative.")
        self._radius = value

# Example usage
circle = Circle(5)
print(circle.radius)    # Output: 5
circle.radius = 10
print(circle.radius)    # Output: 10
# circle.radius = -5    # Raises ValueError: Radius cannot be negative.
```

Key Points:

- The @property decorator allows the method to be accessed as an attribute.

- The @attribute.setter allows setting the value while maintaining control and validation.

- Use **properties** to protect access to internal attributes.

How Do You Implement Multiple Inheritance in Python?

Multiple Inheritance is a feature in Python that allows a class to inherit from more than one parent class. This can be useful for combining behaviors from multiple classes, but it can also lead to complexity (e.g., the Diamond Problem).

Basic Example:

```python
class Base1:
    def greet(self):
        return "Hello from Base1"

class Base2:
    def greet(self):
        return "Hello from Base2"

# Multiple Inheritance
class Derived(Base1, Base2):
    pass

# Example usage
obj = Derived()
print(obj.greet())   # Output: Hello from Base1 (depends on method
resolution order)
```

Method Resolution Order (MRO):

- Determines the order in which classes are searched when looking for a method.

- Use class_name.mro() to see the MRO.

- Python uses the **C3 linearization algorithm** to resolve the order.

Key Takeaways:

- Multiple inheritance should be used cautiously to avoid complexity.

- Understanding MRO is crucial when dealing with multiple inheritance.

How Do You Use Mixin Classes to Add Functionality to Existing Classes?

Mixin Classes are a way to add reusable functionality to classes without using full-blown inheritance. They are typically small classes that provide a specific piece of functionality and are not meant to stand alone.

Mixin Example:

```python
class LogMixin:
    def log(self, message):
```

```
        print(f"Log: {message}")

class Database:
    def connect(self):
        print("Connected to database.")

# Using mixin
class DatabaseLogger(Database, LogMixin):
    pass

# Example usage
db_logger = DatabaseLogger()
db_logger.connect()            # Output: Connected to database.
db_logger.log("Connection established.")  # Output: Log: Connection
established.
```

When to Use Mixins:

- When you need to add behavior without affecting the primary class hierarchy.

- When you have small pieces of functionality that can be reused across different classes.

Best Practices:

- Mixins should be small, specific, and focused on a single responsibility.

- Use clear naming to indicate that a class is a mixin (e.g., LogMixin).

2.3 Functional Programming in Python

What Is Functional Programming, and How Does It Work in Python?

Functional programming (FP) is a programming paradigm where the focus is on using functions and avoiding changing state or mutable data. Python supports functional programming features, allowing developers to write code in a functional style.

Key Concepts:

1. **First-Class Functions**: Functions are treated as first-class citizens, meaning they can be passed as arguments, returned from other functions, and assigned to variables.

94

2. **Pure Functions**: Functions that always produce the same output for the same inputs and have no side effects (don't modify state or rely on external data).

3. **Immutability**: Data does not change once created.

4. **Higher-Order Functions**: Functions that take other functions as parameters or return functions as results.

5. **Recursion**: Using functions that call themselves.

Example:

```python
# First-class function
def greet(name):
    return f"Hello, {name}!"

def process(func, name):
    return func(name)

print(process(greet, "Alice"))  # Output: Hello, Alice!
```

Benefits:

- Easier to debug and test.

- More predictable and readable code.

- Effective use of parallel processing.

How Do You Use map(), filter(), and reduce() in Python?

These are built-in Python functions that support functional programming by applying functions to iterables.

1. **map()**

   The map() function applies a given function to all items in an iterable (e.g., list) and returns a map object (an iterator).

   ```python
   # Example: Squaring a list of numbers
   numbers = [1, 2, 3, 4, 5]
   squared = map(lambda x: x ** 2, numbers)
   print(list(squared))  # Output: [1, 4, 9, 16, 25]
   ```

2. filter()

The filter() function creates an iterator that contains only the elements of the iterable for which the provided function returns True.

```
# Example: Filtering even numbers
numbers = [1, 2, 3, 4, 5, 6]
evens = filter(lambda x: x % 2 == 0, numbers)
print(list(evens))  # Output: [2, 4, 6]
```

3. reduce()

The reduce() function (from functools module) applies a function cumulatively to the items of an iterable, reducing it to a single value.

```
from functools import reduce

# Example: Calculating the product of a list
numbers = [1, 2, 3, 4]
product = reduce(lambda x, y: x * y, numbers)
print(product)  # Output: 24
```

Comparison:

Function	Purpose	Returns
map()	Apply a function to each item in an iterable	Iterator
filter()	Filter items based on a function's condition	Iterator
reduce()	Apply a function cumulatively to reduce an iterable	Single value

What Are Higher-Order Functions in Python, and How Do You Use Them?

A **Higher-Order Function (HOF)** is a function that either:

- Takes one or more functions as arguments, or

- Returns a function as a result.

Examples of Higher-Order Functions:

1. **Taking a Function as an Argument**:

```
def apply_twice(func, value):
    return func(func(value))

# Usage
print(apply_twice(lambda x: x * 2, 5))  # Output: 20
```

2. **Returning a Function**:

```
def make_multiplier(n):
    return lambda x: x * n

doubler = make_multiplier(2)
print(doubler(5))  # Output: 10
```

Built-in Examples:

- map(), filter(), and reduce() are all higher-order functions.

- sorted() can use a function as a key parameter, making it a higher-order function.

Advantages:

- Increase code modularity and reusability.

- Enhance the power of functions by combining behaviors.

What Are Generators and How Do They Improve Memory Efficiency?

A **Generator** is a special type of iterator in Python that generates values one at a time using the yield keyword, instead of returning all values at once. This allows for memory-efficient looping over large datasets.

Creating a Generator:

```
def count_up_to(max_value):
    count = 1
    while count <= max_value:
        yield count  # Pauses function, saves state, and yields value
        count += 1
```

```
# Using the generator
counter = count_up_to(5)
print(next(counter))  # Output: 1
print(next(counter))  # Output: 2
```

Advantages:

- **Memory Efficient**: Generates items on the fly, reducing memory consumption.

- **Lazy Evaluation**: Items are computed only when needed.

- **Infinite Sequences**: Generators can represent infinite sequences without consuming large amounts of memory.

Comparison with List:

```
# Using a list
squares_list = [x ** 2 for x in range(1000000)]  # Memory intensive

# Using a generator expression
squares_gen = (x ** 2 for x in range(1000000))  # Memory efficient
```

How Do You Use Generator Expressions and yield in Python?

Generator Expressions:

Similar to list comprehensions but with parentheses instead of brackets. They return a generator object.

```
# Example: Generator expression for squared numbers
squares = (x ** 2 for x in range(10))
print(next(squares))  # Output: 0
print(next(squares))  # Output: 1
```

Using yield:

The yield keyword is used to turn a function into a generator.

```
def fibonacci_sequence(limit):
    a, b = 0, 1
    while a < limit:
        yield a
        a, b = b, a + b
```

```
# Example usage
fib = fibonacci_sequence(10)
for num in fib:
    print(num)  # Output: 0, 1, 1, 2, 3, 5, 8
```

Key Points:

- Use yield to produce a series of values lazily.

- Generators are ideal for handling large data sets.

How Do You Work With Immutable Data Structures in Python?

Immutable data structures cannot be changed after creation. They help maintain the integrity of data and avoid side effects. Python has several built-in immutable data structures:

Common Immutable Types:

1. **Tuple**:

```
my_tuple = (1, 2, 3)
# my_tuple[0] = 10  # Raises TypeError
```

2. **Frozen Set**:

```
my_set = frozenset([1, 2, 3])
# my_set.add(4)  # Raises AttributeError
```

3. **String**:

```
my_string = "hello"
# my_string[0] = 'H'  # Raises TypeError
```

Why Use Immutability?:

- **Safety**: Reduces unintended modifications.

- **Efficiency**: Immutable objects are easier to optimize.

- **Thread-Safe**: Immutable objects can be safely used in concurrent applications.

Functional Tools for Immutability:

- namedtuple from collections for immutable records.

- tuple and frozenset for fixed data structures.

How Do You Implement Functional Patterns Like Map-Reduce in Python?

Map-Reduce is a popular functional programming pattern for processing and generating data. It consists of two main steps:

1. **Map**: Apply a function to all elements in a collection.

2. **Reduce**: Aggregate results into a single outcome.

Example - Word Count Using Map-Reduce:

1. **Data Preparation**:

```python
text = "Functional programming in Python is powerful and elegant"
words = text.split()
```

2. **Mapping - Count Occurrences of Each Word**:

```python
from collections import Counter
# Map step using Counter
word_count = Counter(words)
print(word_count)  # Output: Counter({'Functional': 1,
'programming': 1, ...})
```

3. **Reducing - Summarizing the Word Counts**:

```python
from functools import reduce
# Reduce step to count the total number of words
total_words = reduce(lambda x, y: x + y, word_count.values())
print(total_words)  # Output: Total count of words
```

Implementing with List Comprehensions:

```python
numbers = [1, 2, 3, 4]
squared_sum = sum(x ** 2 for x in numbers)
print(squared_sum)  # Output: 30
```

Functional Libraries:

- **itertools**: Offers tools like starmap, accumulate, and filterfalse.

- **functools**: Contains reduce and partial.

- **toolz** (third-party library): Provides additional functional tools for iterators and collections.

2.4 Exception Handling and Debugging

How Do You Debug Python Code Using the pdb Module?

pdb Overview:

The pdb module is Python's built-in debugger that allows developers to inspect code, set breakpoints, step through code line-by-line, and evaluate expressions. It is a powerful tool for diagnosing issues during runtime.

Basic Usage:

1. **Starting the Debugger**: Add the following line in your code where you want to start debugging:

```
import pdb; pdb.set_trace()
```

This line will pause the execution and open the pdb interactive mode.

2. **Common Commands in pdb**:

Command	Description
n	Next line (step over)
s	Step into a function
c	Continue execution until the next breakpoint
q	Quit the debugger

l	List the current code
p	Print the value of an expression/variable
b	Set a breakpoint at a specific line

Example:

```python
def calculate_sum(a, b):
    import pdb; pdb.set_trace()  # Start debugging here
    result = a + b
    return result

# Call the function
print(calculate_sum(10, 20))
```

Best Practices:

- Use pdb.set_trace() only during the debugging phase and remove it before deploying code.

- Run the debugger from the terminal using python -m pdb script.py to start debugging from the beginning of the script.

How Do You Log Errors Using Python's logging Module?

logging Overview:

The logging module provides a flexible way to log information about the execution of a program, including errors and warnings. Unlike print(), logging allows you to categorize messages, control output levels, and direct logs to different destinations (console, files, etc.).

Basic Setup:

```python
import logging

# Basic configuration
logging.basicConfig(level=logging.DEBUG, format='%(asctime)s - %(levelname)s - %(message)s')

# Logging messages
```

```
logging.debug("This is a debug message.")
logging.info("Informational message.")
logging.warning("This is a warning.")
logging.error("An error has occurred!")
logging.critical("Critical error!")
```

Log Levels:

1. **DEBUG**: Detailed information, useful for diagnosing problems.

2. **INFO**: General information about program execution.

3. **WARNING**: An indication of something unexpected.

4. **ERROR**: A more serious problem that prevents the program from continuing.

5. **CRITICAL**: A severe error, indicating a critical failure.

Writing Logs to a File:

```
logging.basicConfig(filename='app.log', filemode='w',
level=logging.ERROR)
logging.error("An error occurred in the program.")
```

Best Practices:

- Use logging instead of print statements for tracking program state.

- Separate logs based on severity using log levels.

- Rotate log files using logging.handlers for large applications.

How Do You Handle AssertionError in Python, and When Should You Use assert?

assert Statement:

The assert statement is used to check conditions during development and debugging. If the condition evaluates to False, an AssertionError is raised, which helps catch bugs early.

Basic Usage:

```
def divide(a, b):
    assert b != 0, "Division by zero is not allowed."
```

```
        return a / b

print(divide(10, 2))  # Output: 5.0
# print(divide(10, 0))  # Raises AssertionError: Division by zero is not
allowed.
```

When to Use assert:

- Use assert for debugging purposes to check assumptions and invariants in the code.

- Do **not** use assert for validating user inputs or handling runtime errors. Use exceptions instead.

Handling AssertionError:

To catch and handle AssertionError, use a try-except block:

```
try:
    assert 2 + 2 == 5, "Math error!"
except AssertionError as e:
    print(f"Assertion failed: {e}")
```

How Do You Create Custom Error Classes for More Granular Error Handling?

Creating Custom Exception Classes:

Python allows you to define custom exceptions by inheriting from the Exception class. Custom exceptions provide more specific error handling for complex applications.

Basic Example:

```
class NegativeValueError(Exception):
    """Custom exception for negative values."""
    def __init__(self, value, message="Value cannot be negative"):
        self.value = value
        self.message = f"{message}: {value}"
        super().__init__(self.message)

# Example usage
def calculate_square_root(value):
    if value < 0:
        raise NegativeValueError(value)
    return value ** 0.5
```

104

```
try:
    result = calculate_square_root(-9)
except NegativeValueError as e:
    print(e)  # Output: Value cannot be negative: -9
```

Best Practices:

- Name custom exceptions with the suffix Error to follow convention.

- Inherit from Exception or a built-in error class.

- Use custom exceptions to provide more context in complex error situations.

How Do You Use the traceback Module to Capture Detailed Error Information?

traceback Overview:

The traceback module allows developers to capture and format stack traces of exceptions, which helps in diagnosing problems by providing detailed error information.

Basic Usage:

```
import traceback

def faulty_function():
    return 1 / 0

try:
    faulty_function()
except ZeroDivisionError:
    error_message = traceback.format_exc()  # Capture the stack trace
    print("An error occurred:")
    print(error_message)
```

Key Functions:

1. traceback.print_exc(): Prints the current exception to sys.stderr.

2. traceback.format_exc(): Returns a string representation of the current exception's stack trace.

3. traceback.extract_tb(): Extracts and returns the raw traceback.

105

Use Case:

The traceback module is ideal for logging detailed error information to files or sending stack traces to error-tracking systems.

How Do You Handle Memory Leaks and Performance Bottlenecks in Python Code?

Identifying Memory Leaks:

A **memory leak** occurs when memory that is no longer needed is not released. In Python, memory leaks are rare due to automatic garbage collection, but they can still happen, especially with references to large objects that aren't properly removed.

Tools for Detecting Memory Leaks:

1. **gc Module**: Python's garbage collection module. Use gc.collect() to manually trigger garbage collection.

    ```python
    import gc
    gc.collect()  # Manually trigger garbage collection
    ```

2. **tracemalloc Module**: Tracks memory allocations in Python.

    ```python
    import tracemalloc
    tracemalloc.start()
    # Run some code that might have a memory leak
    snapshot = tracemalloc.take_snapshot()
    top_stats = snapshot.statistics('lineno')
    for stat in top_stats[:10]:
        print(stat)
    ```

Performance Bottlenecks:

Performance bottlenecks can be due to inefficient algorithms or code. Use profiling tools to identify slow parts of the code.

Tools for Identifying Performance Bottlenecks:

1. **cProfile**: A built-in profiler for CPU usage.

    ```python
    import cProfile
    def slow_function():
    ```

```
    sum = 0
    for i in range(1000000):
        sum += i
    return sum
cProfile.run('slow_function()')
```

2. line_profiler (third-party): Profiles memory usage line-by-line.
3. timeit: Measures execution time for small code snippets.

```
import timeit
print(timeit.timeit('"-".join(str(n) for n in range(100))',
number=1000))
```

Best Practices:

- Avoid holding references to large objects that are no longer needed.

- Use generators and lazy evaluation for handling large datasets.

- Optimize algorithms and use efficient data structures.

How Do You Use Breakpoints and Step-Through Debugging in Python IDEs (e.g., PyCharm, VSCode)?

Using Breakpoints:

Breakpoints allow you to pause the execution of your code at a specific line and inspect the current state of variables and objects.

PyCharm:

1. **Setting a Breakpoint**: Click in the left margin next to the line number to set a breakpoint.

2. **Running in Debug Mode**: Use the "Debug" button to run the code in debug mode.

3. **Step Through**: Use the toolbar buttons to:

    ○ **Step Over (F8)**: Move to the next line without diving into functions.

    ○ **Step Into (F7)**: Dive into the function being called.

    ○ **Step Out (Shift+F8)**: Exit the current function and return to the caller.

4. **Viewing Variables**: Use the variable inspector window to monitor variable states.

5. **Evaluate Expressions**: Use the "Evaluate Expression" tool to run code snippets.

VSCode:

1. **Setting a Breakpoint**: Click in the gutter next to the line number to add a breakpoint.

2. **Start Debugging**: Use F5 to start the debug session.

3. **Step Through**:

    ○ **Step Over (F10)**: Step to the next line.

    ○ **Step Into (F11)**: Step into a function.

    ○ **Step Out (Shift+F11)**: Exit the current function.

4. **Watch Panel**: Add variables to the "Watch" panel to monitor their values.

5. **Debug Console**: Use the console to execute commands during the debug session.

Best Practices:

- Use breakpoints strategically to examine specific areas of concern.

- Combine breakpoints with conditional expressions to pause only when certain conditions are met.

- Utilize IDE features like variable watches, evaluation, and stepping tools for thorough inspection.

2.5 Database Access and ORM (Object-Relational Mapping)

How Do You Connect to SQL Databases Using sqlite3 or psycopg2?

Connecting to SQLite Using sqlite3:

SQLite is a lightweight, file-based database system built into Python's standard library via the sqlite3 module.

Basic Example:

```python
import sqlite3
# Connect to SQLite database (or create it if it doesn't exist)
connection = sqlite3.connect('example.db')
cursor = connection.cursor()
# Execute a simple query
cursor.execute('CREATE TABLE IF NOT EXISTS users (id INTEGER PRIMARY KEY, name TEXT)')
connection.commit()
# Close the connection
connection.close()
```

Connecting to PostgreSQL Using psycopg2:

psycopg2 is a popular library for connecting to PostgreSQL databases.

Basic Example:

```python
import psycopg2

# Connect to PostgreSQL database
connection = psycopg2.connect(
    host="localhost",
    database="example_db",
    user="your_username",
    password="your_password"
)
cursor = connection.cursor()

# Execute a simple query
cursor.execute('CREATE TABLE IF NOT EXISTS users (id SERIAL PRIMARY KEY, name TEXT)')
connection.commit()

# Close the connection
cursor.close()
connection.close()
```

Best Practices:

- Use context managers (with statements) to handle connections, ensuring they are properly closed even in case of errors.

- Use parameterized queries to avoid SQL injection.

How Do You Perform CRUD Operations in SQL Databases Using Python?

CRUD (Create, Read, Update, Delete) operations are the basic database actions:

1. **Create:**

```python
import sqlite3

# Create a record
with sqlite3.connect('example.db') as connection:
    cursor = connection.cursor()
    cursor.execute('INSERT INTO users (name) VALUES (?)',
('Alice',))
    connection.commit()
```

2. **Read:**

```python
# Read records
with sqlite3.connect('example.db') as connection:
    cursor = connection.cursor()
    cursor.execute('SELECT * FROM users')
    rows = cursor.fetchall()
    for row in rows:
        print(row)
```

3. **Update:**

```python
# Update a record
with sqlite3.connect('example.db') as connection:
    cursor = connection.cursor()
    cursor.execute('UPDATE users SET name = ? WHERE id = ?',
('Bob', 1))
    connection.commit()
```

4. **Delete**:

```python
# Delete a record
with sqlite3.connect('example.db') as connection:
    cursor = connection.cursor()
    cursor.execute('DELETE FROM users WHERE id = ?', (1,))
    connection.commit()
```

How Do You Use SQLAlchemy for ORM in Python?

SQLAlchemy is a powerful and flexible SQL toolkit and Object-Relational Mapping (ORM) library for Python. It allows you to interact with databases using Python objects instead of SQL queries.

Basic Setup:

1. **Install SQLAlchemy**:

```
pip install sqlalchemy
```

2. **Defining a Model**:

```python
from sqlalchemy import create_engine, Column, Integer, String
from sqlalchemy.ext.declarative import declarative_base
from sqlalchemy.orm import sessionmaker

# Create a database engine
engine = create_engine('sqlite:///example.db')
Base = declarative_base()

# Define a User model
class User(Base):
    __tablename__ = 'users'
    id = Column(Integer, primary_key=True)
    name = Column(String)

# Create tables in the database
Base.metadata.create_all(engine)

# Create a session
Session = sessionmaker(bind=engine)
session = Session()
```

111

3. **CRUD Operations with SQLAlchemy**:

```python
# Create a new user
new_user = User(name="Alice")
session.add(new_user)
session.commit()

# Read users
users = session.query(User).all()
for user in users:
    print(user.name)

# Update a user
user_to_update =
session.query(User).filter_by(name="Alice").first()
user_to_update.name = "Bob"
session.commit()

# Delete a user
session.delete(user_to_update)
session.commit()
```

How Do You Manage Database Migrations Using SQLAlchemy and Alembic?

Alembic is a database migration tool for SQLAlchemy that helps manage changes to the database schema.

Setting Up Alembic:

1. **Install Alembic**:

   ```
   pip install alembic
   ```

2. **Initialize Alembic**:

   ```
   alembic init alembic
   ```

3. This creates an alembic directory with configuration files.

4. **Configure alembic.ini** to point to your database.

5. **Create a Migration**:

```
alembic revision --autogenerate -m "Initial migration"
```

6. **Apply the Migration**:

```
alembic upgrade head
```

Best Practices:

- Use **autogenerate** to detect changes in models automatically.

- Keep migration files in version control for consistency.

How Do You Work With NoSQL Databases (e.g., MongoDB) in Python Using pymongo?

pymongo is a popular library for interacting with MongoDB, a NoSQL database.

Connecting to MongoDB:

1. **Install pymongo**:

```
pip install pymongo
```

2. **Basic Connection**:

```python
from pymongo import MongoClient

# Connect to MongoDB server
client = MongoClient('mongodb://localhost:27017/')
db = client['example_db']
collection = db['users']
```

CRUD Operations with MongoDB:

1. **Create**:

```python
# Insert a document
user = {"name": "Alice", "age": 30}
collection.insert_one(user)
```

2. **Read**:

```python
# Find all documents
users = collection.find()
for user in users:
    print(user)
```

3. **Update**:

```python
# Update a document
collection.update_one({"name": "Alice"}, {"$set": {"age": 31}})
```

4. **Delete**:

```python
# Delete a document
collection.delete_one({"name": "Alice"})
```

What Are Connection Pools, and How Do You Implement Them in Python?

A **connection pool** is a cache of database connections that are reused instead of opening a new connection every time. This improves performance and reduces the overhead of creating new connections.

Using Connection Pool in psycopg2:

```python
from psycopg2 import pool

# Create a connection pool
connection_pool = pool.SimpleConnectionPool(1, 10,
                                            user="your_username",
                                            password="your_password",
                                            host="localhost",
                                            database="example_db")

# Get a connection from the pool
connection = connection_pool.getconn()

# Use the connection
cursor = connection.cursor()
cursor.execute('SELECT * FROM users')
rows = cursor.fetchall()
```

114

```
# Return the connection to the pool
connection_pool.putconn(connection)

# Close the pool
connection_pool.closeall()
```

Best Practices:

- Use connection pools for high-performance applications.

- Limit the maximum number of connections to avoid overloading the database.

How Do You Prevent SQL Injection in Python Database Queries?

SQL Injection is a security vulnerability where an attacker can manipulate SQL queries by injecting malicious code. Use parameterized queries to prevent SQL injection.

Unsafe Example:

```
# Vulnerable to SQL Injection
user_input = "' OR 1=1 --"
cursor.execute(f"SELECT * FROM users WHERE name = '{user_input}'")
```

Safe Example Using Parameterized Queries:

```
# Safe from SQL Injection
user_input = "' OR 1=1 --"
cursor.execute("SELECT * FROM users WHERE name = %s", (user_input,))
```

Best Practices:

- Use parameterized queries (? for SQLite, %s for PostgreSQL).

- Avoid constructing SQL statements with user input directly.

- Validate and sanitize user inputs before processing.

How Do You Optimize SQL Queries in Python for Better Performance?

Optimization Techniques:

1. **Indexing**: Create indexes on columns frequently used in WHERE or JOIN clauses.

```
CREATE INDEX idx_name ON users (name);
```

2. **Limit Result Set**: Use LIMIT to fetch only necessary rows.

```
SELECT * FROM users LIMIT 10;
```

3. **Avoid SELECT ***: Specify columns to reduce data transfer.

```
SELECT id, name FROM users WHERE age > 30;
```

4. **Use JOINs Efficiently**: Use INNER JOIN, LEFT JOIN based on the data requirement.

5. **Avoid N+1 Queries**: Fetch related data in fewer queries using joins or subqueries.

6. **Database Caching**: Implement caching for frequently accessed data.

How Do You Use Indexing and Query Optimization Techniques in Python ORMs?

Indexing in SQLAlchemy:

1. **Define Indexes in Models**:

```python
from sqlalchemy import Index

class User(Base):
    __tablename__ = 'users'
    id = Column(Integer, primary_key=True)
    name = Column(String, index=True)  # Create index on 'name'
column
```

2. **Optimize Queries**:

   ○ Use **lazy loading** for relationships to load related data only when needed.

   ○ Use **eager loading** to load related data in fewer queries using joinedload.

```python
from sqlalchemy.orm import joinedload
users = session.query(User).options(joinedload(User.orders)).all()
```

How Do You Manage Transactions in SQL Databases Using Python?

Transactions Overview:

A **transaction** is a sequence of database operations that are treated as a single unit of work. If any operation fails, the transaction is rolled back to maintain data integrity.

Handling Transactions with sqlite3:

```python
with sqlite3.connect('example.db') as connection:
    cursor = connection.cursor()
    try:
        cursor.execute('BEGIN TRANSACTION')
        cursor.execute('INSERT INTO users (name) VALUES (?)',
('Alice',))
        cursor.execute('INSERT INTO orders (user_id, item) VALUES (?,
?)', (1, 'Book'))
        connection.commit()  # Commit the transaction
    except Exception as e:
        connection.rollback()  # Roll back if any error occurs
        print(f"Transaction failed: {e}")
```

Best Practices:

- Use transactions for multiple related operations to ensure data consistency.

- Always handle exceptions and perform rollbacks when necessary.

How Do You Work With Stored Procedures and Triggers in Python?

Stored Procedures:

Stored procedures are precompiled SQL code stored in the database. They can be called from Python using standard SQL execution methods.

Example Using psycopg2:

```python
# Calling a stored procedure
cursor.execute("CALL update_user_name(%s, %s)", (user_id, new_name))
connection.commit()
```

Triggers:

Triggers are database mechanisms that automatically execute a set of SQL statements when a specific event occurs (e.g., INSERT, UPDATE).

Creating a Trigger:

```
CREATE TRIGGER update_timestamp
AFTER UPDATE ON users
FOR EACH ROW
EXECUTE FUNCTION update_modified_timestamp();
```

Managing Triggers in Python:

Python interacts with triggers indirectly by performing standard SQL operations that trigger the predefined events.

2.6 Web Development with Python

How Do You Build a Simple Web Application Using Flask?

Flask is a lightweight, micro-framework for building web applications in Python. It is minimalistic and easy to set up, making it a popular choice for beginners and small to medium-sized projects.

Installation:

To get started, you need to install Flask:

```
pip install Flask
```

Creating a Simple Flask App:

1. **Create the Flask Application**:

```python
# app.py
from flask import Flask

app = Flask(__name__)

@app.route('/')
```

```
def home():
    return "Hello, Flask!"

if __name__ == '__main__':
    app.run(debug=True)
```

2. **Running the Application**:

```
python app.py
```

Navigate to http://127.0.0.1:5000/ in your web browser to see the "Hello, Flask!" message.

Key Concepts:

- Flask(__name__) initializes a Flask application.

- @app.route('/') is a route decorator to bind URLs to functions.

- app.run(debug=True) starts the server in debug mode for easy development.

What Are the Key Differences Between Flask and Django Web Frameworks?

Flask vs Django:

Feature	Flask	Django
Type	Micro-framework (minimalistic)	Full-stack framework
Flexibility	Highly flexible, add-ons required	Batteries-included, comes with many built-in features
Routing	Simple and explicit	Configurable, uses URL patterns
Database Integration	No built-in ORM, but supports SQLAlchemy	Built-in ORM (Django ORM)
Template Engine	Jinja2 (built-in)	Django Templates
Authentication	Requires extensions (Flask-Login)	Built-in authentication and user management

Learning Curve	Easier to learn, minimal setup	Steeper learning curve, comprehensive setup

When to Use:

- **Flask** is ideal for smaller projects, APIs, and projects where flexibility is required.

- **Django** is best for larger applications that benefit from a structured, opinionated framework.

How Do You Set Up URL Routing in Flask and Django?

URL Routing in Flask:

In Flask, routing is simple and handled using the @app.route() decorator.

Example:

```python
from flask import Flask

app = Flask(__name__)

@app.route('/')  # Root URL
def home():
    return "Home Page"

@app.route('/about')  # About page
def about():
    return "About Page"

@app.route('/user/<username>')  # Dynamic URL with variable
def user_profile(username):
    return f"Hello, {username}!"
```

URL Routing in Django:

In Django, URL routing is defined in the urls.py file. Routes are configured using Django's URL patterns.

Example:

1. **Project-level urls.py:**

```
# project/urls.py
from django.contrib import admin
from django.urls import path
from myapp import views

urlpatterns = [
    path('admin/', admin.site.urls),
    path('', views.home, name='home'),
    path('about/', views.about, name='about'),
    path('user/<str:username>/', views.user_profile,
name='user_profile'),
]
```

2. **View Functions**:

```
# myapp/views.py
from django.http import HttpResponse

def home(request):
    return HttpResponse("Home Page")

def about(request):
    return HttpResponse("About Page")

def user_profile(request, username):
    return HttpResponse(f"Hello, {username}!")
```

Key Differences:

- In **Flask**, routes are defined directly in the code using decorators.

- In **Django**, routing is centralized in urls.py, which adds structure but may feel less flexible.

How Do You Handle GET and POST Requests in a Web Application?

Handling GET and POST in Flask:

In Flask, you use request.method to differentiate between GET and POST requests.

Example:

```
from flask import Flask, request
```

```python
app = Flask(__name__)
@app.route('/form', methods=['GET', 'POST'])
def form():
    if request.method == 'POST':
        data = request.form['input_data']
        return f"Data received: {data}"
    return '''
        <form method="post">
            <input type="text" name="input_data">
            <input type="submit" value="Submit">
        </form>
```

Handling GET and POST in Django:

In Django, you check the request.method attribute in your view function.

Example:

```python
from django.shortcuts import render
from django.http import HttpResponse
def form_view(request):
    if request.method == 'POST':
        data = request.POST.get('input_data')
        return HttpResponse(f"Data received: {data}")
    return render(request, 'form.html')
```

Form Template (form.html):

```html
<form method="post">
    {% csrf_token %}
    <input type="text" name="input_data">
    <input type="submit" value="Submit">
</form>
```

Key Points:

- **Flask**: Use request.form for POST data and request.args for GET parameters.

- **Django**: Use request.POST for POST data and request.GET for GET parameters.

- In Django, **CSRF protection** is enabled by default for forms ({% csrf_token %}).

122

How Do You Manage Templates in Python Web Applications Using Jinja2 or Django Templates?

Jinja2 Templates in Flask:

Jinja2 is the template engine that comes with Flask. It allows you to create dynamic HTML with placeholders.

Example:

1. **Template File** (templates/home.html):

```html
<!doctype html>
<html>
    <head>
        <title>{{ title }}</title>
    </head>
    <body>
        <h1>Welcome, {{ user_name }}!</h1>
    </body>
</html>
```

2. **Render Template in Flask:**

```python
from flask import Flask, render_template

app = Flask(__name__)

@app.route('/')
def home():
    return render_template('home.html', title="Home Page",
user_name="Alice")
```

Django Templates:

Django has its own templating engine, similar to Jinja2, but with a few differences.

Example:

1. **Template File** (templates/home.html):

```html
<!doctype html>
```

```html
<html>
    <head>
        <title>{{ title }}</title>
    </head>
    <body>
        <h1>Welcome, {{ user_name }}!</h1>
    </body>
</html>
```

2. **Render Template in Django**:

```python
from django.shortcuts import render

def home(request):
    context = {'title': 'Home Page', 'user_name': 'Alice'}
    return render(request, 'home.html', context)
```

Template Inheritance:

Both Flask and Django support template inheritance, allowing you to define a base template and extend it for specific pages.

Base Template:

```html
<!-- base.html -->
<!doctype html>
<html>
    <head>
        <title>{% block title %}My Site{% endblock %}</title>
    </head>
    <body>
        <header>{% block header %}{% endblock %}</header>
        <main>{% block content %}{% endblock %}</main>
        <footer>{% block footer %}{% endblock %}</footer>
    </body>
</html>
```

Child Template:

```html
<!-- child.html -->
{% extends "base.html" %}
```

124

```
{% block title %}Home Page{% endblock %}
{% block content %}
    <h1>Welcome to the Home Page!</h1>
{% endblock %}
```

How Do You Serve Static Files and Handle File Uploads in Flask/Django?

Serving Static Files in Flask:

In Flask, you create a static folder in your project to store CSS, JavaScript, and images.

Example:

```html
<!-- HTML Example -->
<link rel="stylesheet" type="text/css" href="{{ url_for('static',
filename='style.css') }}">
<img src="{{ url_for('static', filename='images/logo.png') }}"
alt="Logo">
```

File Upload in Flask:

1. **Form for File Upload**:

```html
<form method="post" enctype="multipart/form-data">
    <input type="file" name="file">
    <input type="submit" value="Upload">
</form>
```

2. **File Handling in Flask**:

```python
from flask import Flask, request
import os

app = Flask(__name__)

@app.route('/upload', methods=['GET', 'POST'])
def upload_file():
    if request.method == 'POST':
        file = request.files['file']
        file.save(os.path.join('uploads', file.filename))
```

```
        return "File uploaded successfully"
    return '''
        <form method="post" enctype="multipart/form-data">
            <input type="file" name="file">
            <input type="submit" value="Upload">
        </form>
    '''
```

Serving Static Files in Django:

1. **Static File Setup** in settings.py:

```
STATIC_URL = '/static/'
STATICFILES_DIRS = [os.path.join(BASE_DIR, 'static')]
```

2. **File Upload in Django:**

   - **Model Setup:**

```
# models.py
from django.db import models

class Document(models.Model):
    upload = models.FileField(upload_to='uploads/')
```

   - **Form for File Upload:**

```
<form method="post" enctype="multipart/form-data">
    {% csrf_token %}
    <input type="file" name="upload">
    <input type="submit" value="Upload">
</form>
```

How Do You Implement Authentication and Authorization in Django Using django.contrib.auth?

Django's built-in authentication system (django.contrib.auth) provides user management, authentication, and authorization features.

Setting Up Authentication:

1. **Create a Superuser**:

```
python manage.py createsuperuser
```

2. **Add django.contrib.auth to INSTALLED_APPS**: Make sure django.contrib.auth and django.contrib.contenttypes are in your INSTALLED_APPS list in settings.py.

3. **User Authentication in Views**:

```python
from django.contrib.auth import authenticate, login, logout
from django.shortcuts import render, redirect
from django.contrib.auth.decorators import login_required

def user_login(request):
    if request.method == 'POST':
        username = request.POST['username']
        password = request.POST['password']
        user = authenticate(request, username=username,
password=password)
        if user is not None:
            login(request, user)
            return redirect('home')
        else:
            return render(request, 'login.html', {'error':
'Invalid credentials'})
    return render(request, 'login.html')

@login_required
def home(request):
    return render(request, 'home.html')
```

4. **Use Authentication Views**: Django provides built-in views for login, logout, and password management:

```python
from django.contrib.auth import views as auth_views
urlpatterns = [
    path('login/', auth_views.LoginView.as_view(), name='login'),
    path('logout/', auth_views.LogoutView.as_view(),
name='logout'),
]
```

5. **Restrict Access**: Use the @login_required decorator to restrict access to authenticated users.

Key Concepts:

- **Authentication**: Verifies the identity of a user.

- **Authorization**: Determines what resources a user is allowed to access.

2.7 API Development and RESTful Services

What Is a RESTful API, and How Do You Build One Using Flask or Django REST Framework?

RESTful API Overview:

A **RESTful API** (Representational State Transfer) is a web service that uses HTTP requests for communication, allowing clients to access and manipulate resources. RESTful APIs are stateless and rely on standard HTTP methods such as:

- **GET**: Retrieve data.

- **POST**: Create new data.

- **PUT/PATCH**: Update existing data.

- **DELETE**: Remove data.

Building a RESTful API Using Flask:

1. **Set Up Flask**:

   ```
   pip install Flask
   ```

2. **Create a Basic API**:

   ```python
   # app.py
   from flask import Flask, jsonify, request

   app = Flask(__name__)
   # In-memory storage for demo purposes
   items = []
   ```

```python
@app.route('/items', methods=['GET'])
def get_items():
    return jsonify(items), 200


@app.route('/items', methods=['POST'])
def add_item():
    new_item = request.json
    items.append(new_item)
    return jsonify(new_item), 201


@app.route('/items/<int:item_id>', methods=['PUT'])
def update_item(item_id):
    if 0 <= item_id < len(items):
        items[item_id] = request.json
        return jsonify(items[item_id]), 200
    return jsonify({'error': 'Item not found'}), 404


@app.route('/items/<int:item_id>', methods=['DELETE'])
def delete_item(item_id):
    if 0 <= item_id < len(items):
        deleted_item = items.pop(item_id)
        return jsonify(deleted_item), 200
    return jsonify({'error': 'Item not found'}), 404


if __name__ == '__main__':
    app.run(debug=True)
```

Building a RESTful API Using Django REST Framework (DRF):

1. **Set Up Django REST Framework**:

```
pip install djangorestframework
```

2. **Add DRF to INSTALLED_APPS** in settings.py:

```python
INSTALLED_APPS = [
    ...,
    'rest_framework',
]
```

129

3. **Create a Simple API**:

- **Create a Model**:

```python
# models.py
from django.db import models

class Item(models.Model):
    name = models.CharField(max_length=100)
    description = models.TextField()
```

- **Create a Serializer**:

```python
# serializers.py
from rest_framework import serializers
from .models import Item

class ItemSerializer(serializers.ModelSerializer):
    class Meta:
        model = Item
        fields = '__all__'
```

- **Create a View**:

```python
# views.py
from rest_framework import viewsets
from .models import Item
from .serializers import ItemSerializer

class ItemViewSet(viewsets.ModelViewSet):
    queryset = Item.objects.all()
    serializer_class = ItemSerializer
```

- **Set Up Routing**:

```python
# urls.py
from django.urls import path, include
from rest_framework.routers import DefaultRouter
from .views import ItemViewSet

router = DefaultRouter()
```

```
router.register(r'items', ItemViewSet)

urlpatterns = [
    path('api/', include(router.urls)),
]
```

How Do You Use requests for Making HTTP Calls in Python?

The requests library is a popular HTTP library in Python used to interact with APIs.

Installation:

```
pip install requests
```

Basic Example:

```python
import requests
# Making a GET request
response = requests.get('https://jsonplaceholder.typicode.com/posts/1')
if response.status_code == 200:
    data = response.json()
    print(data)
# Making a POST request
payload = {'title': 'New Post', 'body': 'This is a new post', 'userId': 1}
response = requests.post('https://jsonplaceholder.typicode.com/posts', json=payload)
print(response.json())
```

Key Features:

- Use requests.get() for GET requests.

- Use requests.post() for POST requests with json or data parameters.

- Access **response status** with response.status_code.

- Parse **JSON responses** with response.json().

131

How Do You Implement Rate Limiting and Throttling for APIs?

Rate Limiting controls the number of requests a client can make in a specific time window to prevent abuse and ensure fair usage.

Flask Rate Limiting:

Use the Flask-Limiter extension for implementing rate limits.

```
pip install Flask-Limiter
```

Example:

```python
from flask import Flask
from flask_limiter import Limiter

app = Flask(__name__)
limiter = Limiter(app, key_func=lambda: "global")  # Simple global rate
limit

@app.route('/resource')
@limiter.limit("5 per minute")  # Limit to 5 requests per minute
def limited_resource():
    return "This resource is rate limited."

if __name__ == '__main__':
    app.run(debug=True)
```

Django Rate Limiting:

Django REST Framework has built-in throttling support.

1. **Configure Throttling** in settings.py:

```python
REST_FRAMEWORK = {
    'DEFAULT_THROTTLE_CLASSES': [
        'rest_framework.throttling.UserRateThrottle',
    ],
    'DEFAULT_THROTTLE_RATES': {
        'user': '5/minute',  # 5 requests per minute per user
    }
}
```

How Do You Secure APIs Using OAuth2 or JSON Web Tokens (JWT)?

OAuth2:

OAuth2 is a standard protocol for authorization that allows third-party services to access user resources without exposing credentials.

Using OAuth2 with Django:

1. **Install django-oauth-toolkit:**

   ```
   pip install django-oauth-toolkit
   ```

2. **Add to INSTALLED_APPS:**

   ```
   INSTALLED_APPS = [
       ...,
       'oauth2_provider',
   ]
   ```

3. **Configure OAuth2**: Use the OAuth2 Provider with Django REST Framework to secure endpoints.

JSON Web Tokens (JWT):

JWT is a compact and self-contained token used for securely transmitting information.

Using JWT with Django:

1. **Install djangorestframework-simplejwt:**

   ```
   pip install djangorestframework-simplejwt
   ```

2. **Configure JWT in settings.py:**

   ```
   REST_FRAMEWORK = {
       'DEFAULT_AUTHENTICATION_CLASSES': (

   'rest_framework_simplejwt.authentication.JWTAuthentication',
       ),
   }
   ```

3. **Set Up Token Endpoints**:

```python
from django.urls import path
from rest_framework_simplejwt.views import (
    TokenObtainPairView,
    TokenRefreshView,
)
urlpatterns = [
    path('api/token/', TokenObtainPairView.as_view(),
name='token_obtain_pair'),
    path('api/token/refresh/', TokenRefreshView.as_view(),
name='token_refresh'),
]
```

How Do You Design and Version APIs for Long-Term Maintenance?

API Versioning is crucial for managing changes and updates without breaking existing clients. There are several ways to version an API:

Common Versioning Strategies:

1. **URI Versioning**:

```
/api/v1/items/
/api/v2/items/
```

2. **Header Versioning**: Use custom headers like Accept:

```
Accept: application/vnd.example.v1+json
```

3. **Query Parameter Versioning**:

```
/api/items?version=1
```

Implementing Versioning in Django REST Framework:

1. **Settings Configuration**:

```python
REST_FRAMEWORK = {
    'DEFAULT_VERSIONING_CLASS':
'rest_framework.versioning.URLPathVersioning',
}
```

2. **URL Configuration**:

```
Копировать код
from django.urls import path, include

urlpatterns = [
    path('api/v1/', include('myapp.v1_urls')),
    path('api/v2/', include('myapp.v2_urls')),
]
```

What Is API Documentation, and How Do You Generate It Using Swagger/OpenAPI?

API Documentation describes the endpoints, methods, parameters, and responses of an API, making it easier for developers to understand and use the API.

Using Swagger/OpenAPI with Flask:

1. **Install flask-swagger-ui**:

```
pip install flask-swagger-ui
```

2. **Setup Example**:

```
from flask import Flask, jsonify
from flask_swagger_ui import get_swaggerui_blueprint

app = Flask(__name__)

SWAGGER_URL = '/swagger'
API_URL = '/static/swagger.json'
swagger_ui = get_swaggerui_blueprint(SWAGGER_URL, API_URL)
app.register_blueprint(swagger_ui, url_prefix=SWAGGER_URL)

@app.route('/items', methods=['GET'])
def get_items():
    return jsonify([])

if __name__ == '__main__':
    app.run(debug=True)
```

Using Swagger/OpenAPI with Django:

1. **Install** drf-yasg (Yet Another Swagger Generator):

```
pip install drf-yasg
```

2. **Setup in** urls.py:

```python
from rest_framework import permissions
from drf_yasg.views import get_schema_view
from drf_yasg import openapi
from django.urls import path
schema_view = get_schema_view(
    openapi.Info(
        title="My API",
        default_version='v1',
    ),
    public=True,
    permission_classes=(permissions.AllowAny,),
)
urlpatterns = [
    path('swagger/', schema_view.with_ui('swagger',
cache_timeout=0), name='schema-swagger-ui'),
]
```

How Do You Handle Cross-Origin Resource Sharing (CORS) in Python Web Applications?

CORS (Cross-Origin Resource Sharing) is a security feature implemented by browsers to control how web pages can make requests to different domains. It prevents unauthorized requests between different origins.

Enabling CORS in Flask:

1. **Install** Flask-CORS:

```
pip install flask-cors
```

2. **Setup Example**:

```python
from flask import Flask
```

```python
from flask_cors import CORS
app = Flask(__name__)
CORS(app)  # Enable CORS for all routes
@app.route('/data')
def data():
    return {'key': 'value'}
```

Enabling CORS in Django:

1. **Install django-cors-headers:**

```
pip install django-cors-headers
```

2. **Add to INSTALLED_APPS and Configure in settings.py:**

```python
INSTALLED_APPS = [
    ...,
    'corsheaders',
]
MIDDLEWARE = [
    'corsheaders.middleware.CorsMiddleware',
    ...,
]
# Allow all origins (for testing purposes only)
CORS_ALLOW_ALL_ORIGINS = True
```

3. **Restrict Origins:**

```python
CORS_ALLOWED_ORIGINS = [
    "https://example.com",
    "https://anotherdomain.com",
]
```

Best Practices:

- Use CORS_ALLOW_ALL_ORIGINS = True only for development/testing.

- Restrict allowed origins to trusted domains in production.

2.8 File Processing and Serialization

How Do You Read and Write CSV Files Using the csv Module?

The csv module in Python provides functionality to handle **Comma-Separated Values (CSV)** files, which are widely used for data storage and exchange.

Reading CSV Files:

To read CSV files, use the csv.reader() or DictReader().

Example Using csv.reader():

```python
import csv

# Reading a CSV file
with open('example.csv', mode='r') as file:
    csv_reader = csv.reader(file)
    for row in csv_reader:
        print(row)
```

Example Using DictReader():

```python
# Reading a CSV file as a dictionary
with open('example.csv', mode='r') as file:
    csv_reader = csv.DictReader(file)
    for row in csv_reader:
        print(row)  # Each row is a dictionary with column headers as
keys
```

Writing CSV Files:

To write CSV files, use the csv.writer() or DictWriter().

Example Using csv.writer():

```python
# Writing to a CSV file
with open('output.csv', mode='w', newline='') as file:
    csv_writer = csv.writer(file)
```

```
csv_writer.writerow(['Name', 'Age', 'City'])
csv_writer.writerow(['Alice', '30', 'New York'])
csv_writer.writerow(['Bob', '25', 'San Francisco'])
```

Example Using DictWriter():

```
# Writing a CSV file from a dictionary
with open('output.csv', mode='w', newline='') as file:
    fieldnames = ['Name', 'Age', 'City']
    csv_writer = csv.DictWriter(file, fieldnames=fieldnames)
    csv_writer.writeheader()
    csv_writer.writerow({'Name': 'Alice', 'Age': '30', 'City': 'New
York'})
    csv_writer.writerow({'Name': 'Bob', 'Age': '25', 'City': 'San
Francisco'})
```

How Do You Work With JSON Data in Python Using the json Module?

The json module in Python provides an easy way to work with **JavaScript Object Notation (JSON)** data, a popular format for data exchange between applications.

Reading JSON Data:

Use json.load() to read JSON data from a file and json.loads() to read from a string.

Example:

```
import json

# Reading JSON data from a file
with open('data.json', 'r') as file:
    data = json.load(file)
    print(data)  # Output: Parsed JSON as a Python dictionary

# Reading JSON from a string
json_string = '{"name": "Alice", "age": 30, "city": "New York"}'
data = json.loads(json_string)
print(data)
```

Writing JSON Data:

Use json.dump() to write JSON data to a file and json.dumps() to convert a Python object to a JSON string.

Example:

```python
# Writing JSON data to a file
data = {'name': 'Alice', 'age': 30, 'city': 'New York'}
with open('data.json', 'w') as file:
    json.dump(data, file, indent=4)  # Indent for pretty printing

# Converting a Python object to a JSON string
json_string = json.dumps(data, indent=4)
print(json_string)
```

Best Practices:

- Use indent in json.dump() for better readability.

- Handle errors with try-except blocks for JSON parsing.

How Do You Use the pickle Module for Object Serialization and Deserialization?

The pickle module in Python is used for **serializing and deserializing** Python objects (converting them to a byte stream and back).

Serialization (Pickling):

To serialize an object, use pickle.dump() for files or pickle.dumps() for a string of bytes.

Example:

```python
import pickle

# Creating an object
data = {'name': 'Alice', 'age': 30, 'city': 'New York'}

# Serializing (pickling) the object
with open('data.pkl', 'wb') as file:
    pickle.dump(data, file)
```

Deserialization (Unpickling):

To deserialize an object, use pickle.load() for files or pickle.loads() for a byte string.

Example:

```
# Deserializing (unpickling) the object
with open('data.pkl', 'rb') as file:
    data = pickle.load(file)
    print(data)  # Output: {'name': 'Alice', 'age': 30, 'city': 'New
York'}
```

Best Practices:

- Be cautious when loading data from untrusted sources, as pickle can execute arbitrary code.

- Consider alternatives like **JSON** or **MessagePack** for safer serialization.

How Do You Parse and Process XML Data Using xml.etree.ElementTree?

The xml.etree.ElementTree module provides tools to parse and create **XML** documents in Python.

Parsing XML:

To parse XML, use ElementTree.parse() for files or ElementTree.fromstring() for strings.

Example:

```
import xml.etree.ElementTree as ET

# Parsing XML from a file
tree = ET.parse('data.xml')
root = tree.getroot()

# Accessing elements
for child in root:
    print(child.tag, child.attrib)
```

Creating XML:

To create XML, use ElementTree.Element() and ElementTree.SubElement().

Example:

```
# Creating an XML document
root = ET.Element("people")
person = ET.SubElement(root, "person", attrib={"id": "1"})
name = ET.SubElement(person, "name")
name.text = "Alice"

# Writing to a file
tree = ET.ElementTree(root)
tree.write("output.xml")
```

Best Practices:

- Use find() and findall() methods to search for specific elements.

- Use iter() for iterating over elements.

How Do You Work With YAML Files Using PyYAML?

YAML is a human-readable data format that is often used for configuration files. The PyYAML library allows you to read and write YAML files in Python.

Installation:

```
pip install pyyaml
```

Reading YAML Files:

Use yaml.safe_load() to read YAML data from a file.

Example:

```
import yaml

# Reading YAML data from a file
with open('config.yaml', 'r') as file:
    config = yaml.safe_load(file)
    print(config)  # Output: Parsed YAML as a Python dictionary
```

Writing YAML Files:

Use yaml.safe_dump() to write data to a YAML file.

Example:

```
# Writing data to a YAML file
data = {'name': 'Alice', 'age': 30, 'city': 'New York'}
with open('config.yaml', 'w') as file:
    yaml.safe_dump(data, file)
```

Best Practices:

- Use yaml.safe_load() instead of yaml.load() to avoid security risks.

- Prefer YAML for configuration files due to its readability.

How Do You Compress and Decompress Files Using zipfile and gzip Modules?

Python provides built-in libraries for handling file compression and decompression, including zipfile for ZIP files and gzip for GZIP files.

Using zipfile:

- **Creating a ZIP File:**

```
import zipfile

# Creating a ZIP file
with zipfile.ZipFile('example.zip', 'w') as zipf:
    zipf.write('file1.txt')
    zipf.write('file2.txt')
```

- **Extracting a ZIP File:**

```
# Extracting a ZIP file
with zipfile.ZipFile('example.zip', 'r') as zipf:
    zipf.extractall('extracted_files')
```

Using gzip:

- **Compressing a File:**

```
import gzip

# Compressing a file
with open('example.txt', 'rb') as f_in:
```

143

```
    with gzip.open('example.txt.gz', 'wb') as f_out:
        f_out.writelines(f_in)
```

- **Decompressing a File:**

```
# Decompressing a file
with gzip.open('example.txt.gz', 'rb') as f_in:
    with open('decompressed.txt', 'wb') as f_out:
        f_out.write(f_in.read())
```

Best Practices:

- Use **ZIP** for multi-file compression.

- Use **GZIP** for single-file compression with better compression ratio.

How Do You Handle Binary Data in Python Files?

Binary data refers to data that is not encoded as text, like images or executable files. Python provides methods to handle binary data using file modes like 'rb' (read binary) or 'wb' (write binary).

Reading Binary Data:

```
# Reading binary data
with open('example.bin', 'rb') as file:
    binary_data = file.read()
    print(binary_data)
```

Writing Binary Data:

```
# Writing binary data
data = b'\x89PNG\r\n\x1a\n\x00\x00\x00\rIHDR\x00\x00\x01\x00'
with open('output.bin', 'wb') as file:
    file.write(data)
```

Handling Binary Data in Images:

Use the **PIL** (Pillow) library for processing image files:

```
pip install Pillow
```

Example Using Pillow:

```python
from PIL import Image

# Opening an image file
with open('example.jpg', 'rb') as file:
    img = Image.open(file)
    img.show()

# Saving an image as binary
img.save('output.png', format='PNG')
```

Best Practices:

- Always open binary files with 'rb' or 'wb' modes to avoid encoding issues.

- Use specialized libraries like **Pillow** for handling complex binary formats like images.

2.9 Concurrency and Multithreading

How Do You Use the threading Module for Multithreaded Applications?

The threading module in Python provides a simple way to create and manage threads, enabling multiple operations to occur simultaneously.

Creating and Starting Threads:

Use threading.Thread to create and start a thread.

Example:

```python
import threading

# Define a simple function for the thread
def print_numbers():
    for i in range(5):
        print(f"Number: {i}")

# Create and start a thread
```

```
thread = threading.Thread(target=print_numbers)
thread.start()

# Wait for the thread to complete
thread.join()
print("Thread has finished execution.")
```

Key Concepts:

- **threading.Thread(target=...)**: Creates a new thread with the target function.

- **start()**: Starts the thread's execution.

- **join()**: Blocks the calling thread until the thread finishes execution.

Extending the Thread Class:

```
class MyThread(threading.Thread):
    def run(self):
        for i in range(5):
            print(f"Thread number: {i}")
# Create and start the custom thread
thread = MyThread()
thread.start()
thread.join()
```

Use Cases:

- Useful for **I/O-bound** tasks (e.g., reading files, network operations) where the program waits for external data.

What Is the Global Interpreter Lock (GIL), and How Does It Affect Python Multithreading?

Global Interpreter Lock (GIL):

The **GIL** is a mutex that allows only one thread to execute Python bytecode at a time, even in a multithreaded program. This means that Python threads are not truly parallel in **CPU-bound** tasks.

Impact of GIL:

- **CPU-bound tasks** (heavy computations): GIL can be a bottleneck because threads are not executed in parallel.

146

- **I/O-bound tasks** (network, file I/O): GIL has less impact, as threads can yield control while waiting for I/O operations.

Why Does Python Have GIL?

- Memory management in CPython (default implementation of Python) relies on reference counting, which is protected by the GIL.

- Removing the GIL could complicate memory management and reduce single-threaded performance.

Alternatives to GIL:

- Use the multiprocessing module to achieve true parallelism by creating separate processes, each with its own GIL.

- Use alternative Python implementations (e.g., **Jython**, **IronPython**) that do not have a GIL.

How Do You Manage Threads Using ThreadPoolExecutor from the concurrent.futures Module?

The concurrent.futures module provides a high-level API for asynchronously executing callables. ThreadPoolExecutor is used to manage a pool of threads.

Basic Usage:

```python
from concurrent.futures import ThreadPoolExecutor

def square(x):
    return x * x

# Create a ThreadPoolExecutor with 5 worker threads
with ThreadPoolExecutor(max_workers=5) as executor:
    results = executor.map(square, range(10))

# Print the results
print(list(results))  # Output: [0, 1, 4, 9, 16, 25, 36, 49, 64, 81]
```

Key Concepts:

- max_workers: Sets the number of threads in the pool.

- submit(): Submits a callable to be executed, returns a Future object.

- map(): Executes a function over an iterable, returns results as they are completed.

- result(): Retrieves the result from a Future.

Example Using submit():

```
with ThreadPoolExecutor(max_workers=3) as executor:
    future1 = executor.submit(square, 2)
    future2 = executor.submit(square, 3)

    # Retrieve results
    print(future1.result())  # Output: 4
    print(future2.result())  # Output: 9
```

Use Cases:

- Ideal for managing **concurrent I/O-bound** tasks efficiently.

- Use ThreadPoolExecutor for easier thread management without manually handling thread lifecycle.

How Do You Use the multiprocessing Module for Parallel Execution?

The multiprocessing module in Python is used to create separate processes that run concurrently, bypassing the GIL and achieving true parallelism.

Creating and Managing Processes:

Use multiprocessing.Process to create and manage processes.

Example:

```
from multiprocessing import Process

# Function to be executed in a process
def print_numbers():
    for i in range(5):
        print(f"Process number: {i}")

# Create and start a process
process = Process(target=print_numbers)
process.start()
```

```
# Wait for the process to finish
process.join()
print("Process has finished execution.")
```

Using Pool for Process Management:

The Pool class is used to manage multiple worker processes.

Example:

```
from multiprocessing import Pool

def square(x):
    return x * x

# Create a pool with 4 processes
with Pool(processes=4) as pool:
    results = pool.map(square, range(10))

print(results)  # Output: [0, 1, 4, 9, 16, 25, 36, 49, 64, 81]
```

Key Concepts:

- **Process**: Create and manage individual processes.

- **Pool**: Manage a pool of worker processes, making it easier to parallelize tasks.

- **Queue**: A thread- and process-safe way to share data between processes.

Use Cases:

- Use multiprocessing for **CPU-bound** tasks (e.g., heavy computations, data processing) to take advantage of multiple cores.

How Do You Share Data Safely Between Threads Using Locks and Queues?

Using Locks:

A **Lock** is a synchronization primitive that prevents multiple threads from accessing a shared resource simultaneously, ensuring data integrity.

Example:

```
import threading

# Shared resource
counter = 0
lock = threading.Lock()

def increment():
    global counter
    for _ in range(10000):
        with lock:  # Acquire the lock before modifying the shared resource
            counter += 1

# Create and start threads
threads = [threading.Thread(target=increment) for _ in range(10)]
for thread in threads:
    thread.start()
for thread in threads:
    thread.join()

print(f"Final counter value: {counter}")
```

Using Queues:

A **Queue** is a thread-safe data structure that can be used for communication between threads.

Example:

```
import threading
from queue import Queue

# Create a thread-safe queue
queue = Queue()

# Producer function
def producer():
    for i in range(5):
        queue.put(i)
        print(f"Produced {i}")
```

```
# Consumer function
def consumer():
    while not queue.empty():
        item = queue.get()
        print(f"Consumed {item}")

# Create and start threads
producer_thread = threading.Thread(target=producer)
consumer_thread = threading.Thread(target=consumer)
producer_thread.start()
producer_thread.join()
consumer_thread.start()
consumer_thread.join()
```

Key Concepts:

- **Lock**: Use lock.acquire() and lock.release() or a context manager (with lock) to ensure safe access.

- **Queue**: Use queue.put() to add items and queue.get() to remove items. It handles synchronization automatically.

How Do You Handle Synchronization Issues in Multithreaded Programs?

Synchronization issues occur when multiple threads try to access shared resources concurrently, leading to inconsistent results or unpredictable behavior.

Techniques to Handle Synchronization:

1. **Locks**: Use Lock to ensure that only one thread accesses a critical section at a time.

   - **Problem**: Can lead to **deadlocks** if not managed carefully.

2. **RLocks**: Use RLock (reentrant lock) when a thread needs to acquire the same lock multiple times.

   ```
   lock = threading.RLock()
   ```

3. **Semaphores**: Use Semaphore to control access to a resource for a limited number of threads.

   ```
   semaphore = threading.Semaphore(3)  # Allow 3 threads to access
   simultaneously
   ```

151

4. **Events**: Use Event to coordinate threads, allowing one thread to wait until another signals completion.

```
event = threading.Event()
event.wait()  # Wait until the event is set
```

5. **Condition Variables**: Use Condition to wait for a specific condition to become true before proceeding.

```
condition = threading.Condition()
with condition:
    condition.wait()  # Wait for a notification
```

What Are Race Conditions, and How Do You Prevent Them?

Race Conditions:

A **race condition** occurs when two or more threads attempt to modify shared data simultaneously, leading to inconsistent or unexpected results. The outcome of the program depends on the timing of thread execution, making it difficult to predict.

Example of a Race Condition:

```
import threading

counter = 0

def increment():
    global counter
    for _ in range(10000):
        counter += 1

# Create and start threads
threads = [threading.Thread(target=increment) for _ in range(10)]
for thread in threads:
    thread.start()
for thread in threads:
    thread.join()

print(f"Final counter value: {counter}")  # Inconsistent result
```

152

Preventing Race Conditions:

1. **Use Locks**:

```python
lock = threading.Lock()

def increment():
    global counter
    for _ in range(10000):
        with lock:
            counter += 1
```

2. **Avoid Shared State**:

   - Use local variables whenever possible to minimize shared data between threads.

   - Use thread-safe data structures like **Queue**.

3. **Use Higher-Level Concurrency Tools**:

   - Use concurrent.futures and multiprocessing for better abstractions.

   - Use ThreadPoolExecutor for managing tasks without manually handling locks.

Best Practices:

- Avoid fine-grained locking as it can lead to complex code and deadlocks.

- Use thread-safe data structures like **Queue** or high-level tools like ThreadPoolExecutor.

- Carefully test multithreaded code for race conditions and use logging for debugging.

2.10 Asynchronous Programming

What Is Asynchronous Programming, and How Is It Different From Multithreading?

Asynchronous Programming Overview:

Asynchronous programming allows the program to perform other tasks while waiting for long-running operations (like I/O) to complete. It is useful for handling multiple I/O-bound tasks efficiently,

153

such as network requests, file I/O, and database operations, without blocking the main execution thread.

Key Differences Between Asynchronous Programming and Multithreading:

Feature	Asynchronous Programming	Multithreading
Execution	Single-threaded, cooperative multitasking	Multiple threads running concurrently
Performance	Ideal for I/O-bound tasks	Suitable for both I/O-bound and CPU-bound
GIL Impact	Avoids Global Interpreter Lock (GIL) issues	Affected by GIL, limiting true parallelism
Complexity	Simpler to manage with async/await	Complexity increases with synchronization
Blocking	Non-blocking	Threads can block each other if not managed

Use Cases:

- Use **asynchronous programming** for I/O-bound tasks (network operations, database queries).

- Use **multithreading** for concurrent tasks that may involve I/O and light CPU work.

- Use **multiprocessing** for CPU-bound tasks to take advantage of multiple cores.

How Do You Use the asyncio Module for Writing Asynchronous Code?

asyncio Overview:

The asyncio module provides tools for writing **asynchronous code** using async and await keywords. It includes an event loop that schedules and manages asynchronous tasks.

Basic Example:

```
import asyncio

# Define an asynchronous function
```

154

```python
async def say_hello():
    print("Hello...")
    await asyncio.sleep(2)   # Simulate an I/O-bound task
    print("...World!")

# Run the coroutine
asyncio.run(say_hello())
```

Key Concepts:

- **async def**: Defines an asynchronous function (coroutine).

- **await**: Pauses the coroutine and waits for the result of another coroutine.

- **asyncio.run()**: Executes the asynchronous function until completion.

How Do You Work With async and await in Python Functions?

async and **await** **Keywords:**

- **async** is used to define a coroutine, a special type of function that can be paused and resumed.

- **await** is used to pause the execution of a coroutine until the awaited coroutine completes.

Example:

```python
import asyncio

# Asynchronous function
async def fetch_data():
    print("Fetching data...")
    await asyncio.sleep(3)   # Simulate a network request
    return {"data": "Sample data"}

# Another asynchronous function
async def main():
    result = await fetch_data()   # Wait until fetch_data completes
    print(f"Data received: {result}")

# Run the main coroutine
asyncio.run(main())
```

Key Takeaways:

- await can only be used inside async functions.

- An async **function** returns a coroutine object, which must be awaited to get the result.

How Do You Create and Manage Event Loops in asyncio?

Event Loop Overview:

An **event loop** is a core component of asyncio. It is responsible for executing asynchronous tasks and managing their scheduling.

Creating and Accessing Event Loops:

1. **Create and Run an Event Loop**:

```python
import asyncio

async def hello():
    print("Hello, World!")

# Create an event loop
loop = asyncio.new_event_loop()
asyncio.set_event_loop(loop)

# Run the coroutine within the loop
loop.run_until_complete(hello())
loop.close()
```

2. **Default Event Loop**:

```python
# Access the current event loop
loop = asyncio.get_event_loop()
loop.run_until_complete(hello())
```

Managing Event Loops:

- run_until_complete(): Runs a coroutine until it completes.

- run_forever(): Keeps the event loop running indefinitely.

- stop() and close(): Stops and closes the event loop.

156

Best Practices:

- Prefer using **asyncio.run()** for simple cases instead of manually creating and managing loops.

- Use **await** instead of manually scheduling tasks for better readability.

How Do You Use aiohttp for Asynchronous HTTP Requests?

aiohttp is an asynchronous HTTP client and server framework. It is commonly used to make non-blocking HTTP requests.

Installation:

```
pip install aiohttp
```

Example of Asynchronous HTTP Request:

```python
import aiohttp
import asyncio

# Asynchronous function to fetch data
async def fetch_url(url):
    async with aiohttp.ClientSession() as session:
        async with session.get(url) as response:
            data = await response.text()
            print(f"Data from {url}: {data[:100]}...")  # Display first
100 characters

# Main function to run multiple requests
async def main():
    urls = ['https://jsonplaceholder.typicode.com/posts/1',
            'https://jsonplaceholder.typicode.com/posts/2']
    tasks = [fetch_url(url) for url in urls]
    await asyncio.gather(*tasks)

# Run the main function
asyncio.run(main())
```

Key Concepts:

- **ClientSession**: Manages the HTTP session.

- **session.get()**: Performs an asynchronous GET request.

- Use **await** for non-blocking I/O operations (like fetching data).

How Do You Handle Asynchronous Tasks Using asyncio.gather() and asyncio.wait()?

asyncio.gather():

- Collects multiple asynchronous tasks and runs them concurrently.

- Returns results as a list in the order they were provided.

- **Example:**

```python
import asyncio

# Define multiple asynchronous tasks
async def task1():
    await asyncio.sleep(2)
    return "Task 1 Complete"

async def task2():
    await asyncio.sleep(1)
    return "Task 2 Complete"

# Run tasks concurrently
async def main():
    results = await asyncio.gather(task1(), task2())
    print(results)  # Output: ['Task 1 Complete', 'Task 2
Complete']

asyncio.run(main())
```

asyncio.wait():

- Waits for multiple tasks to complete, with more control over when tasks are considered finished.

- Supports waiting for **all** or **any** tasks to complete.

158

- **Example:**

```python
# Wait for tasks using asyncio.wait()
async def main():
    tasks = [task1(), task2()]
    done, pending = await asyncio.wait(tasks)
    for task in done:
        print(task.result())
asyncio.run(main())
```

Key Differences:

- gather(): Returns results directly in a list.

- wait(): Separates completed (done) and incomplete (pending) tasks.

How Do You Manage Timeouts and Error Handling in Asynchronous Code?

Handling Timeouts:

Use asyncio.wait_for() to set a timeout for an asynchronous operation.

Example:

```python
import asyncio

# Simulate a long-running task
async def long_running_task():
    await asyncio.sleep(5)
    return "Task Complete"

# Run the task with a timeout
async def main():
    try:
        result = await asyncio.wait_for(long_running_task(), timeout=2)
# 2-second timeout
    except asyncio.TimeoutError:
        result = "Task Timed Out!"
    print(result)

asyncio.run(main())  # Output: Task Timed Out!
```

Error Handling in Asynchronous Code:

Use try-except blocks inside asynchronous functions to handle errors gracefully.

Example:

```python
import aiohttp

# Asynchronous function with error handling
async def fetch_data(url):
    try:
        async with aiohttp.ClientSession() as session:
            async with session.get(url) as response:
                if response.status != 200:
                    raise Exception(f"Failed to fetch {url}")
                data = await response.text()
                return data
    except Exception as e:
        print(f"Error: {e}")

# Main function to fetch data
async def main():
    url = 'https://invalid-url'
    await fetch_data(url)  # This will raise an exception

asyncio.run(main())
```

Best Practices:

- Use **asyncio.wait_for()** for setting timeouts.

- Use try-except blocks within **asynchronous functions** to handle exceptions.

- Properly manage **cancellation** with asyncio.CancelledError.

Managing Task Cancellation:

```python
async def cancellable_task():
    try:
        while True:
            print("Running...")
            await asyncio.sleep(1)
```

```
        except asyncio.CancelledError:
            print("Task was cancelled.")
            raise
# Main function to demonstrate cancellation
async def main():
    task = asyncio.create_task(cancellable_task())
    await asyncio.sleep(3)  # Let the task run for 3 seconds
    task.cancel()           # Cancel the task
    try:
        await task
    except asyncio.CancelledError:
        print("Caught task cancellation.")
asyncio.run(main())
```

2.11 Testing and Debugging

How Do You Write and Organize Unit Tests in pytest?

What is pytest?

pytest is a popular testing framework for Python that is known for its simplicity and powerful features. It allows you to write small, scalable tests and includes features for fixtures, parameterized testing, and plugins.

Installation:

```
pip install pytest
```

Writing Basic Tests:

1. Create a test file (e.g., test_example.py).

2. Write functions prefixed with test_.

Example:

```
# my_module.py
def add(a, b):
```

```
    return a + b
# test_example.py
from my_module import add
def test_add():
    assert add(2, 3) == 5
    assert add(-1, 1) == 0
```

Running Tests:

```
pytest test_example.py
```

Organizing Tests:

- **Create a tests/ directory**: Store all test files inside a folder.

- **Test file names** should be prefixed with test_.

- Use **modules** and **subfolders** for organizing larger projects.

Parameterized Testing:

You can use @pytest.mark.parametrize to run a test with multiple sets of inputs.

```
import pytest
@pytest.mark.parametrize("a,b,expected", [
    (2, 3, 5),
    (-1, 1, 0),
    (0, 0, 0)
])
def test_add(a, b, expected):
    assert add(a, b) == expected
```

How Do You Use unittest.mock for Mocking in Python Tests?

What is unittest.mock?

unittest.mock is a library for mocking objects in Python. Mocking allows you to replace parts of the system under test with mock objects and make assertions about how they are used.

Mocking a Function:

Replace a function call with a mock during a test

.

162

Example:

```python
from unittest.mock import patch
import my_module

# Mocking my_module's external API call
@patch('my_module.external_api_call')
def test_function(mock_api):
    mock_api.return_value = {'status': 'success'}

    result = my_module.some_function()

    # Assertions
    mock_api.assert_called_once()  # Ensure it was called once
    assert result == 'success'
```

Using MagicMock:

MagicMock is a more powerful version of a mock, supporting magic methods like __getitem__ and __call__.

Example:

```python
from unittest.mock import MagicMock

mock_object = MagicMock()
mock_object.some_method.return_value = "mocked value"

assert mock_object.some_method() == "mocked value"
```

Mocking Classes:

Mock a whole class to replace its methods and attributes.

```python
# Mocking a class
with patch('my_module.MyClass') as MockClass:
    instance = MockClass.return_value
    instance.method.return_value = 'mocked result'
    # Use the mock in the test
    result = instance.method()
    assert result == 'mocked result'
```

163

How Do You Perform Integration Testing in a Web Application?

What is Integration Testing?

Integration testing verifies that different components of a system work together as expected. In web applications, this often involves testing APIs, database interactions, and the application's end-to-end behavior.

Tools for Integration Testing:

1. pytest with plugins like pytest-django for Django apps.

2. requests or httpx for HTTP requests in Flask/Django.

3. **Django Test Framework**: Use Django's built-in TestCase.

Integration Testing Example with Django:

1. **Set Up**: Create test files using Django's built-in testing tools.

2. **Example**:

```python
from django.test import TestCase
from django.urls import reverse
from .models import Item
class ItemIntegrationTest(TestCase):
    def setUp(self):
        Item.objects.create(name="Test Item", description="Test
Description")
    def test_item_list_view(self):
        response = self.client.get(reverse('item-list'))
        self.assertEqual(response.status_code, 200)
        self.assertContains(response, "Test Item")
```

Integration Testing Example with Flask:

1. **Setup**: Use Flask's test_client.

2. **Example**:

```python
from my_app import app
def test_home_page():
    with app.test_client() as client:
        response = client.get('/')
```

```
    assert response.status_code == 200
    assert b"Welcome" in response.data
```

How Do You Use Test Fixtures in pytest for Reusable Test Setup?

What are Fixtures?

Fixtures in pytest provide a fixed baseline for tests. They are reusable pieces of code that set up the required context before running the actual test.

Creating a Fixture:

Use the @pytest.fixture decorator.

Example:

```python
import pytest

# Define a fixture for database setup
@pytest.fixture
def sample_data():
    # Setup code
    data = {'name': 'Alice', 'age': 30}
    return data

# Use the fixture in a test
def test_data(sample_data):
    assert sample_data['name'] == 'Alice'
    assert sample_data['age'] == 30
```

Fixture Scope:

- function (default): Fixture is run once per test.

- module: Run once per module.

- session: Run once per test session.

```python
@pytest.fixture(scope="module")
def setup_database():
    # Setup code here
    yield  # Code after yield will run after tests
```

How Do You Automate Testing and Generate Test Coverage Reports?

Automating Tests with pytest**:**

1. Run all tests automatically using:

    ```
    pytest
    ```

2. To watch for file changes, use **pytest-watch**:

    ```
    pip install pytest-watch
    ptw   # Run pytest with auto-reload
    ```

Generating Test Coverage Reports:

Use the coverage library to check how much of the code is covered by tests.

Installation:

```
pip install coverage
```

Basic Usage:

1. **Run Tests with Coverage**:

    ```
    coverage run -m pytest
    ```

2. **Generate and View Report**:

    ```
    coverage report
    coverage html   # Create an HTML report
    ```

3. **View HTML Report**: Open htmlcov/index.html in a browser to see detailed coverage.

How Do You Perform Load Testing for Python Web Applications Using Tools Like Locust?

What is Load Testing?

Load testing checks how an application behaves under heavy usage or high traffic, identifying bottlenecks and performance issues.

Using Locust for Load Testing:

Locust is a performance testing tool for load testing web applications.

Installation:

```
pip install locust
```

Basic Locust File (locustfile.py):

```python
from locust import HttpUser, TaskSet, task

class MyTasks(TaskSet):
    @task
    def index_page(self):
        self.client.get("/")

    @task
    def about_page(self):
        self.client.get("/about")

class WebsiteUser(HttpUser):
    tasks = [MyTasks]
    min_wait = 1000   # Minimum wait time between tasks (ms)
    max_wait = 5000   # Maximum wait time between tasks (ms)
```

Running Locust:

1. Start the Locust server:

   ```
   locust
   ```

2. Navigate to http://localhost:8089 in your browser.

3. Enter the number of users and spawn rate, then start the test.

167

Key Metrics:

- **Requests per second.**

- **Response time.**

- **Failure rate.**

How Do You Debug Complex Python Applications Using the pdb Debugger?

What is pdb?

pdb is Python's built-in interactive debugger. It allows you to set breakpoints, step through code, inspect variables, and evaluate expressions.

Basic Commands:

Command	Description
b	Set a breakpoint (e.g., b 10 for line 10)
s	Step into a function
n	Step to the next line
c	Continue execution until the next breakpoint
l	List the source code around the current line
p	Print the value of a variable
q	Quit the debugger

Using pdb:

1. Add import pdb; pdb.set_trace() in the code where you want to start debugging.

2. Run the script, and the debugger will activate at the breakpoint.

Example:

```python
def divide(a, b):
    import pdb; pdb.set_trace()  # Start debugging here
    return a / b

divide(10, 0)  # This will raise an exception
```

Using pdb in the Command Line:

```python
python -m pdb script.py
```

Best Practices:

- Use breakpoints sparingly in production code; remove them after debugging.

- Use **conditional breakpoints** with b followed by a condition (e.g., b 15, x == 5).

Advanced Debugging Tools:

- ipdb: An improved version of pdb with better navigation.

- pudb: A full-screen console-based visual debugger.

- **Integrated Debugging in IDEs**: Tools like PyCharm and VSCode provide advanced debugging features, including breakpoints, watches, and variable inspection.

Section 3: Advanced Questions

3.1 Design Patterns in Python

How Do You Implement the Singleton Design Pattern in Python?

What is the Singleton Pattern?

The **Singleton** design pattern ensures that a class has only one instance and provides a global point of access to that instance. This is useful when exactly one object is needed to coordinate actions across the system.

Implementation in Python:

1. **Using a Class Method**:

```python
class Singleton:
    _instance = None

    @classmethod
    def get_instance(cls):
        if cls._instance is None:
            cls._instance = cls()
        return cls._instance

# Usage
singleton1 = Singleton.get_instance()
singleton2 = Singleton.get_instance()
print(singleton1 is singleton2)  # Output: True
```

2. **Using a Decorator**:

```python
def singleton(cls):
    instances = {}

    def get_instance(*args, **kwargs):
        if cls not in instances:
            instances[cls] = cls(*args, **kwargs)
        return instances[cls]
```

172

```
        return get_instance
@singleton
class SingletonClass:
    pass


# Usage
obj1 = SingletonClass()
obj2 = SingletonClass()
print(obj1 is obj2)   # Output: True
```

3. **Using __new__ Method**:

```
class Singleton:
    _instance = None

    def __new__(cls, *args, **kwargs):
        if not cls._instance:
            cls._instance = super().__new__(cls)
        return cls._instance


# Usage
s1 = Singleton()
s2 = Singleton()
print(s1 is s2)   # Output: True
```

How Do You Use the Factory Method Pattern to Create Objects in Python?

What is the Factory Method Pattern?

The **Factory Method** pattern defines an interface for creating an object but lets subclasses alter the type of objects that will be created. This pattern is useful when the exact type of object isn't known until runtime.

Implementation in Python:

```
from abc import ABC, abstractmethod


# Abstract product
class Button(ABC):
    @abstractmethod
```

```python
    def render(self):
        pass
# Concrete products
class WindowsButton(Button):
    def render(self):
        return "Rendering a button in Windows style."


class MacOSButton(Button):
    def render(self):
        return "Rendering a button in MacOS style."


# Factory class
class ButtonFactory:
    def create_button(self, os_type):
        if os_type == "Windows":
            return WindowsButton()
        elif os_type == "MacOS":
            return MacOSButton()
        else:
            raise ValueError("Unknown OS type")


# Usage
factory = ButtonFactory()
button = factory.create_button("Windows")
print(button.render())  # Output: Rendering a button in Windows style.
```

Benefits:

- Allows creation of objects without specifying the exact class.

- Encourages loose coupling between client code and object creation.

What Is the Observer Pattern, and How Do You Implement It in Python?

What is the Observer Pattern?

The **Observer** pattern defines a one-to-many dependency between objects so that when one object changes state, all its dependents are notified automatically. It's often used in implementing distributed event-handling systems.

Implementation in Python:

```python
# Subject class
class Subject:
    def __init__(self):
        self._observers = []

    def register_observer(self, observer):
        self._observers.append(observer)

    def notify_observers(self, message):
        for observer in self._observers:
            observer.update(message)

# Observer interface
class Observer:
    def update(self, message):
        pass

# Concrete observer
class ConcreteObserver(Observer):
    def update(self, message):
        print(f"Received message: {message}")

# Usage
subject = Subject()
observer1 = ConcreteObserver()
observer2 = ConcreteObserver()

subject.register_observer(observer1)
subject.register_observer(observer2)

subject.notify_observers("Event occurred!")  # Both observers will
receive the message.
```

Benefits:

- Promotes loose coupling between the subject and observers.

- Useful for implementing **event-driven** architectures.

175

How Do You Use the Decorator Pattern for Extending Functionality in Python?

What is the Decorator Pattern?

The **Decorator** pattern allows behavior to be added to individual objects, dynamically, without affecting the behavior of other objects from the same class. It's used for adhering to the **Open/Closed Principle**.

Implementation in Python:

1. **Using a Function Decorator**:

```python
def bold_decorator(func):
    def wrapper():
        return f"<b>{func()}</b>"
    return wrapper
@bold_decorator
def greet():
    return "Hello, World!"
# Usage
print(greet())  # Output: <b>Hello, World!</b>
```

2. **Class-Based Decorator**:

```python
class BoldDecorator:
    def __init__(self, function):
        self.function = function
    def __call__(self):
        return f"<b>{self.function()}</b>"
@BoldDecorator
def greet():
    return "Hello, World!"
# Usage
print(greet())  # Output: <b>Hello, World!</b>
```

Benefits:

- More flexible than inheritance for adding responsibilities.

- Avoids monolithic class hierarchies.

How Do You Apply the Strategy Pattern to Choose Between Different Algorithms?

What is the Strategy Pattern?

The **Strategy** pattern defines a family of algorithms, encapsulates each one, and makes them interchangeable. This pattern lets the algorithm vary independently from the clients that use it.

Implementation in Python:

```python
from abc import ABC, abstractmethod

# Strategy interface
class SortStrategy(ABC):
    @abstractmethod
    def sort(self, data):
        pass

# Concrete strategies
class QuickSort(SortStrategy):
    def sort(self, data):
        return sorted(data)  # Python's built-in sort (quick sort)

class BubbleSort(SortStrategy):
    def sort(self, data):
        # Simple bubble sort implementation
        n = len(data)
        for i in range(n):
            for j in range(0, n-i-1):
                if data[j] > data[j+1]:
                    data[j], data[j+1] = data[j+1], data[j]
        return data

# Context class
class SortContext:
    def __init__(self, strategy: SortStrategy):
        self._strategy = strategy

    def set_strategy(self, strategy: SortStrategy):
        self._strategy = strategy
```

```
    def sort_data(self, data):
        return self._strategy.sort(data)

# Usage
data = [5, 2, 9, 1, 5, 6]
context = SortContext(QuickSort())
print(context.sort_data(data))   # Uses QuickSort

context.set_strategy(BubbleSort())
print(context.sort_data(data))   # Uses BubbleSort
```

Benefits:

- Allows algorithms to be selected at runtime.

- Encapsulates algorithm details, promoting cleaner and more maintainable code.

How Do You Implement the Proxy and Adapter Design Patterns in Python?

What is the Proxy Pattern?

The **Proxy** pattern provides a surrogate or placeholder for another object to control access to it. Common uses include logging, access control, and lazy initialization.

Implementation in Python:

```
class RealSubject:
    def request(self):
        print("Request handled by RealSubject.")

class Proxy:
    def __init__(self):
        self._real_subject = RealSubject()

    def request(self):
        # Additional logic (e.g., access control)
        print("Proxy: Checking access before handling the request.")
        self._real_subject.request()

# Usage
```

```
proxy = Proxy()
proxy.request()
```

What is the Adapter Pattern?

The **Adapter** pattern allows objects with incompatible interfaces to work together by creating an intermediary that adapts one interface to another.

Implementation in Python:

```python
class EuropeanSocket:
    def voltage(self):
        return 230


class USASocket:
    def voltage(self):
        return 120


# Adapter class
class SocketAdapter:
    def __init__(self, european_socket):
        self.european_socket = european_socket

    def voltage(self):
        return self.european_socket.voltage() / 2  # Convert to 120V


# Usage
european_socket = EuropeanSocket()
adapter = SocketAdapter(european_socket)
print(f"Adapted voltage: {adapter.voltage()}V")  # Output: 115V
```

Benefits:

- **Proxy**: Controls access and adds additional behavior without changing the original object.

- **Adapter**: Makes incompatible systems compatible without modifying their source code.

What Is the Command Pattern, and How Do You Use It in Python Applications?

What is the Command Pattern?

The **Command** pattern turns a request into a stand-alone object that contains all information about the request. This allows you to parameterize methods, delay or queue a request's execution, and support undoable operations.

Implementation in Python:

```python
# Command interface
class Command(ABC):
    @abstractmethod
    def execute(self):
        pass

# Concrete commands
class LightOnCommand(Command):
    def __init__(self, light):
        self.light = light

    def execute(self):
        self.light.turn_on()

class LightOffCommand(Command):
    def __init__(self, light):
        self.light = light

    def execute(self):
        self.light.turn_off()

# Receiver
class Light:
    def turn_on(self):
        print("Light is ON")

    def turn_off(self):
        print("Light is OFF")

# Invoker
class RemoteControl:
    def __init__(self):
        self._commands = []
```

```python
    def set_command(self, command):
        self._commands.append(command)

    def execute_commands(self):
        for command in self._commands:
            command.execute()

# Usage
light = Light()
light_on = LightOnCommand(light)
light_off = LightOffCommand(light)

remote = RemoteControl()
remote.set_command(light_on)
remote.set_command(light_off)
remote.execute_commands()
```

Benefits:

- Encapsulates requests as objects, allowing flexible and dynamic command execution.

- Makes it easy to implement **undo/redo** functionality.

3.2 Advanced OOP and Metaprogramming

What Is Metaprogramming, and How Do You Use It in Python?

What is Metaprogramming?

Metaprogramming refers to the ability of a program to manipulate itself or another program during runtime. In Python, metaprogramming is primarily achieved using:

- **Metaclasses**: Classes that define the behavior of other classes.

- **Decorators**: Functions that modify other functions or classes.

- **Reflection and Introspection**: Tools to examine and modify objects at runtime.

Example - Function Decorator:

```python
def uppercase_decorator(func):
    def wrapper():
        result = func()
        return result.upper()
    return wrapper
@uppercase_decorator
def greet():
    return "Hello, World!"

# Usage
print(greet())   # Output: HELLO, WORLD!
```

Example - Metaclass:

```python
# Define a metaclass
class MyMeta(type):
    def __new__(cls, name, bases, dct):
        dct['greet'] = lambda self: "Hello from metaclass!"
        return super().__new__(cls, name, bases, dct)

# Use the metaclass in a class
class MyClass(metaclass=MyMeta):
    pass

# Usage
obj = MyClass()
print(obj.greet())   # Output: Hello from metaclass!
```

Benefits:

- Allows for **dynamic class creation**.

- Enhances flexibility by modifying code behavior at runtime.

- Reduces repetitive code through reusable patterns.

How Do You Create Custom Metaclasses in Python, and What Are Their Uses?

What Are Metaclasses?

A **metaclass** is a class of a class that defines how classes behave. A class in Python is itself an object, and a metaclass is what creates these class objects. Metaclasses are useful when you want to control the creation of classes.

Creating a Custom Metaclass:

```python
class MyMeta(type):
    def __new__(cls, name, bases, dct):
        # Modify class attributes during creation
        dct['class_attribute'] = 'Added by MyMeta'
        return super().__new__(cls, name, bases, dct)

# Class using MyMeta as its metaclass
class MyClass(metaclass=MyMeta):
    def __init__(self):
        self.instance_attribute = 'Original'

# Usage
obj = MyClass()
print(obj.class_attribute)  # Output: Added by MyMeta
```

Use Cases:

- **Enforcing class-level constraints** (e.g., all methods must be implemented).

- **Automatically registering subclasses**.

- **Adding or modifying class attributes**.

Key Metaclass Methods:

- __new__(cls, name, bases, dct): Called to create the class object.

- __init__(cls, name, bases, dct): Initializes the class object.

- __call__(cls, *args, **kwargs): Invoked when a class instance is created.

What Are Python's Dunder (Magic) Methods, and How Do You Override Them (e.g., __new__, __call__)?

What Are Dunder Methods?

Dunder (double underscore) or **magic methods** are special methods with double underscores that define the behavior of objects for built-in operations (e.g., addition, string representation).

Common Dunder Methods:

Method	Purpose
__init__	Initializes an object (constructor)
__new__	Creates a new instance of a class
__str__	Returns a human-readable string representation of an object
__repr__	Returns a developer-friendly string representation of an object
__call__	Makes an instance callable like a function
__getitem__	Allows index access (e.g., obj[index])

Overriding __new__ and __call__:

1. __new__: Controls object creation before initialization.

```python
class MyClass:
    def __new__(cls, *args, **kwargs):
        instance = super().__new__(cls)
        instance.value = 42
        return instance

    def __init__(self, name):
        self.name = name

# Usage
obj = MyClass("Example")
```

184

```
    print(obj.name)    # Output: Example
    print(obj.value)   # Output: 42
```

2. __call__: Makes an instance callable like a function.

```
    class CallableClass:
        def __init__(self, value):
            self.value = value
        def __call__(self):
            return f"Called with value {self.value}"
    # Usage
    obj = CallableClass(10)
    print(obj())  # Output: Called with value 10
```

Use Cases:

- __new__: Useful in **singleton pattern** to control object creation.

- __call__: Often used to create **function-like objects**.

How Do You Use Reflection and Introspection in Python to Modify Classes at Runtime?

Reflection and Introspection:

- **Introspection** is the ability to examine the type or properties of an object at runtime.

- **Reflection** is the ability to manipulate the structure of an object or class at runtime.

Using getattr and setattr:

- getattr(object, name): Returns the value of an attribute.

- setattr(object, name, value): Sets the value of an attribute.

Example:

```
class MyClass:
    def __init__(self):
        self.name = "Initial"

# Introspection
obj = MyClass()
```

```
print(getattr(obj, 'name'))  # Output: Initial

# Reflection
setattr(obj, 'name', 'Modified')
print(obj.name)  # Output: Modified
```

Using hasattr and dir:

- **hasattr(object, name)**: Checks if an attribute exists.

- **dir(object)**: Returns a list of attributes and methods.

Example:

```
# Check if 'name' attribute exists
if hasattr(obj, 'name'):
    print("Attribute 'name' exists.")

# List all attributes and methods
print(dir(obj))
```

Use Cases:

- **Dynamically adding attributes** to objects.

- **Modifying class behavior** during runtime.

- Creating **flexible frameworks** that can adapt to changing requirements.

How Do You Dynamically Add Attributes and Methods to Python Objects?

Dynamically Adding Attributes:

You can use setattr() to add attributes to an instance at runtime.

Example:

```
class MyClass:
    pass

obj = MyClass()
setattr(obj, 'dynamic_attribute', 42)
print(obj.dynamic_attribute)  # Output: 42
```

Dynamically Adding Methods:

You can assign functions to an object's attribute to add methods dynamically.

Example:

```python
def dynamic_method(self):
    return "Dynamic Method Called"

# Adding method to a class instance
obj.dynamic_method = dynamic_method.__get__(obj)
print(obj.dynamic_method())   # Output: Dynamic Method Called
```

Use Cases:

- Extending object functionality at runtime.

- **Monkey patching**: Altering modules or classes in runtime.

- Implementing **plugins or dynamic behavior**.

How Do You Implement Custom Descriptors and Property Methods in Python?

What are Descriptors?

Descriptors are objects that define how an attribute is accessed and modified. A descriptor must implement one or more of the following methods:

- __get__(self, instance, owner): Retrieves the attribute value.

- __set__(self, instance, value): Sets the attribute value.

- __delete__(self, instance): Deletes the attribute.

Example of a Descriptor:

```python
class IntegerDescriptor:
    def __init__(self, name):
        self.name = name

    def __get__(self, instance, owner):
        return instance.__dict__.get(self.name)

    def __set__(self, instance, value):
```

187

```
        if not isinstance(value, int):
            raise ValueError("Value must be an integer")
        instance.__dict__[self.name] = value

class MyClass:
    age = IntegerDescriptor('age')

# Usage
obj = MyClass()
obj.age = 25
print(obj.age)    # Output: 25
# obj.age = "string"    # Raises ValueError
```

Using @property Decorator:

The **@property** decorator is a built-in way to define **getter**, **setter**, and **deleter** methods for an attribute.

Example:

```
class Person:
    def __init__(self, name):
        self._name = name

    @property
    def name(self):
        return self._name

    @name.setter
    def name(self, value):
        if not value:
            raise ValueError("Name cannot be empty")
        self._name = value

# Usage
person = Person("Alice")
print(person.name)    # Output: Alice
person.name = "Bob"    # Set new name
```

Use Cases:

- Enforcing **data validation**.

- Creating **computed attributes**.

- Controlling attribute **access behavior**.

How Do You Leverage Python's __slots__ for Memory Optimization in Object-Oriented Code?

What is __slots__?

The __slots__ attribute in a class limits the attributes that objects can have, preventing the creation of a __dict__ and thereby reducing memory usage. This is useful for optimizing memory when dealing with a large number of instances.

Implementation of __slots__:

```python
class OptimizedClass:
    __slots__ = ['name', 'age']
    def __init__(self, name, age):
        self.name = name
        self.age = age
# Usage
obj = OptimizedClass("Alice", 30)
# obj.address = "Unknown"  # Raises AttributeError due to the use of
__slots__
```

Benefits:

- **Memory Efficiency**: Reduces memory usage by eliminating the __dict__.

- **Faster Attribute Access**: Accessing attributes is faster when using __slots__.

Limitations:

- No dynamic attribute creation (only attributes defined in __slots__ are allowed).

- Inheritance with __slots__ can be tricky, requiring explicit definition in subclasses.

Use Cases:

- **High-performance applications** with many instances.

- **Memory-constrained environments**.

189

3.3 Memory Management and Optimization

How Does Python Handle Memory Management and Garbage Collection Internally?

Memory Management in Python:

Python uses an automatic memory management system, which includes a built-in garbage collector. Here are the key components:

1. **Heap Memory**: All Python objects and data structures are stored in a private heap. This is managed by the Python memory manager.

2. **Reference Counting**: Python uses **reference counting** to keep track of the number of references to an object. When an object's reference count drops to zero, it is deallocated.

   - sys.getrefcount(obj) can be used to check an object's reference count.

Garbage Collection:

Python also uses a **cyclic garbage collector** to handle reference cycles (when two or more objects reference each other, creating a loop):

- The garbage collector identifies and cleans up circular references that the reference counting system can't handle.

- The garbage collector is part of the gc module and runs periodically.

Example:

```python
import gc
import sys

# Example of reference counting
a = []
print(sys.getrefcount(a))  # Output: Reference count of a

# Example of circular reference
class Node:
    def __init__(self, value):
```

```
        self.value = value
        self.next = None

node1 = Node(1)
node2 = Node(2)
node1.next = node2
node2.next = node1   # Circular reference
```

How Do You Use the gc Module to Control Garbage Collection?

The gc module provides an interface to interact with the garbage collector. You can enable, disable, and manually trigger garbage collection using this module.

Key Functions:

1. gc.enable(): Enables the garbage collector.

2. gc.disable(): Disables the garbage collector.

3. gc.collect(): Manually triggers garbage collection.

4. gc.get_threshold(): Returns the current collection thresholds.

5. gc.set_threshold(thresholds): Sets new collection thresholds.

Example:

```
import gc

# Disable automatic garbage collection
gc.disable()
# Perform some operations
# Manually trigger garbage collection
gc.collect()
# Re-enable garbage collection
gc.enable()
```

Best Practices:

- Avoid disabling garbage collection unless necessary.

- Use gc.collect() in memory-intensive applications to forcefully clean up circular references.

- Adjust gc.set_threshold() for fine-tuning based on your application's needs.

191

How Do You Profile Memory Usage in a Python Application Using memory_profiler or tracemalloc?

Using memory_profiler:

memory_profiler is a third-party library used for monitoring memory usage line by line.

Installation: pip install memory-profiler

Basic Usage:

1. **Add the @profile decorator** to the function you want to monitor.

2. Run the script using python -m memory_profiler script.py.

Example:

```python
from memory_profiler import profile

@profile
def memory_intensive_function():
    data = [x * x for x in range(1000000)]  # Memory-intensive operation
    return data

memory_intensive_function()
```

Using tracemalloc:

tracemalloc is a built-in module that tracks memory allocation over time, allowing you to compare snapshots of memory usage.

Example:

```python
import tracemalloc

# Start tracing memory
tracemalloc.start()

# Take snapshots
snapshot1 = tracemalloc.take_snapshot()

# Perform memory-intensive operations
data = [x * x for x in range(1000000)]
```

```
# Take another snapshot
snapshot2 = tracemalloc.take_snapshot()

# Compare snapshots
stats = snapshot2.compare_to(snapshot1, 'lineno')
for stat in stats[:5]:
    print(stat)
```

Key Metrics:

- **Peak memory usage.**

- **Memory leaks.**

- **Top memory consumers.**

What Are Common Causes of Memory Leaks in Python, and How Do You Prevent Them?

Common Causes of Memory Leaks:

1. **Unintentional Circular References**: Objects reference each other, preventing garbage collection.

   o **Solution**: Use weak references to break cycles.

2. **Global Variables**: Holding large data in global variables can lead to memory bloat.

   o **Solution**: Limit the use of global variables and use local scope.

3. **Large Caches**: Using large caches that are not properly managed can lead to memory exhaustion.

   o **Solution**: Implement cache eviction policies (e.g., LRU - Least Recently Used).

4. **Open File Descriptors**: Forgetting to close files after opening them can cause memory leaks.

   o **Solution**: Use context managers (with statement) to manage resources.

Example - Circular Reference Solution:

```
import weakref
```

```
class Node:
    def __init__(self, value):
        self.value = value
        self.next = None

# Use a weak reference to break the cycle
node1 = Node(1)
node2 = Node(2)
node1.next = weakref.ref(node2)
node2.next = weakref.ref(node1)
```

Tools to Detect Memory Leaks:

- **gc module**: Use gc.get_objects() to track all objects.

- **objgraph**: A third-party library for visualizing object references.

How Do You Use Weak References to Manage Memory More Efficiently?

What Are Weak References?

A **weak reference** allows you to reference an object without increasing its reference count. This means the garbage collector can reclaim the object even if a weak reference to it exists.

Using weakref Module:

1. **weakref.ref()**: Creates a weak reference to an object.

2. **weakref.WeakKeyDictionary**: A dictionary where keys are weak references.

3. **weakref.WeakValueDictionary**: A dictionary where values are weak references.

Example:

```
import weakref

class MyClass:
    pass

# Create an instance and a weak reference
obj = MyClass()
weak_obj = weakref.ref(obj)
```

```
# Check if the object is still alive
print(weak_obj())  # Output: <__main__.MyClass object at 0x...>
del obj
print(weak_obj())  # Output: None (object has been garbage collected)
```

Use Cases:

- **Cache management**.

- **Breaking reference cycles**.

- Managing objects that are **temporarily needed**.

How Do You Optimize Data Structures for Memory Usage in Large Applications?

Optimizing Data Structures:

1. **Use Generators Instead of Lists**: Generators use **lazy evaluation**, generating values on the fly without storing them in memory.

   Example:

   ```
   # List comprehension (memory-intensive)
   data = [x * x for x in range(1000000)]
   # Generator expression (memory-efficient)
   data_gen = (x * x for x in range(1000000))
   ```

2. **Use array Module Instead of Lists**: If storing large collections of numbers, use the array module for efficient memory usage.

   Example:

   ```
   from array import array
   # Integer array (memory-efficient)
   numbers = array('i', [1, 2, 3, 4, 5])
   ```

3. **Use collections.deque for Queues**: Use deque from collections for efficient queue operations.

Example:

```
from collections import deque
queue = deque()
queue.append('item')
queue.popleft()  # Faster than list pop(0)
```

4. **Use __slots__ to Avoid __dict__**: Use __slots__ in classes to limit memory usage by avoiding the dynamic creation of instance dictionaries.

Example:

```
class OptimizedClass:
    __slots__ = ['name', 'age']
```

5. **Choose the Right Data Structure**:

   ○ Use **set** for membership checks.

   ○ Use **deque** for efficient pop/append operations.

   ○ Use **numpy** arrays for numerical computations.

How Do You Minimize the Memory Footprint of an Application That Processes Large Datasets?

Strategies for Minimizing Memory Usage:

1. **Streaming Data Processing**: Process data in chunks instead of loading everything into memory at once.

Example:

```
# Process a large file line by line
with open('large_file.txt', 'r') as file:
    for line in file:
        process(line)
```

2. **Use pandas with chunksize**: When working with large datasets in pandas, use the chunksize parameter to load data in smaller parts.

Example:

```python
import pandas as pd
for chunk in pd.read_csv('large_dataset.csv', chunksize=10000):
    process(chunk)
```

3. **Use numpy for Memory-Efficient Arrays**: numpy arrays are more memory-efficient than Python lists.

   Example:

```python
import numpy as np
data = np.array([1, 2, 3, 4, 5], dtype=np.int32)  # Memory-
efficient
```

4. **Use In-Place Operations**: Perform operations in-place when possible to reduce memory overhead.

   Example:

```python
data = [1, 2, 3, 4, 5]
data.sort()  # In-place sorting, instead of creating a new list
```

5. **Compression**: Use compression to store data more efficiently.

   Use the zlib or gzip modules for compressing and decompressing data.

6. **Memory Mapping with mmap**: Use memory-mapped files for large datasets to avoid loading the entire dataset into memory.

   Example:

```python
import mmap
with open('large_file.dat', 'r+b') as f:
    mmapped_file = mmap.mmap(f.fileno(), 0)
    print(mmapped_file.readline())
```

Best Practices:

- Always use **generators** for large data processing.

- **Profile and optimize** critical memory hotspots using tools like memory_profiler.

- Choose the **appropriate data structure** for the task to avoid unnecessary memory overhead.

197

3.4 Performance Optimization

How Do You Profile and Optimize CPU-Bound and I/O-Bound Tasks in Python?

Profiling CPU-Bound Tasks

CPU-bound tasks are those that use a lot of processing power, like complex computations or data transformations. The goal is to optimize code to use CPU resources efficiently.

Example - Using cProfile for CPU-Bound Tasks:

```python
import cProfile
# CPU-bound example: Factorial calculation
def factorial(n):
    if n == 0 or n == 1:
        return 1
    return n * factorial(n - 1)
# Profile the function
cProfile.run('factorial(20)')
```

Optimizing CPU-Bound Code

- Use **efficient algorithms** to reduce computational complexity.

- **Avoid recursion** when possible to prevent stack overflow; prefer iterative solutions.

- **Leverage multithreading** (though it is limited by the Global Interpreter Lock (GIL) for CPU-bound tasks) or, better, use **multiprocessing** for true parallelism.

Profiling I/O-Bound Tasks

I/O-bound tasks involve operations that wait for external events like file I/O, database queries, or network requests. Use asynchronous programming or concurrency to improve performance.

Example - Using timeit for I/O-Bound Tasks:

```python
import timeit

# I/O-bound example: Reading a file
def read_file():
```

```python
    with open('large_file.txt', 'r') as f:
        data = f.read()
    return data

# Measure execution time
execution_time = timeit.timeit(read_file, number=5)
print(f"Execution time: {execution_time} seconds")
```

Optimizing I/O-Bound Code

- Use **asynchronous I/O** with asyncio.

- Implement **batch processing** for database queries.

- Use **caching** to avoid repetitive I/O operations.

What Is the Role of the cProfile Module in Optimizing Performance?

cProfile Overview

cProfile is a built-in Python module that allows you to profile your code and gather detailed performance statistics. It measures the time spent in each function, the number of calls, and can highlight the bottlenecks in your code.

How to Use cProfile:

1. **Profile a Function:**

```python
import cProfile

def example_function():
    total = 0
    for i in range(100000):
        total += i
    return total

# Profile the function
cProfile.run('example_function()')
```

2. **Save Profile to a File:**

```python
# Save profiling results to a file
```

```
profiler = cProfile.Profile()
profiler.enable()
example_function()
profiler.disable()
profiler.dump_stats('profile_output.prof')
```

3. **Analyze Profile with pstats**

```
import pstats

# Load and print profile data
with open('profile_output.prof', 'rb') as f:
    stats = pstats.Stats(f)
    stats.sort_stats('time').print_stats(10)  # Top 10 functions
by time
```

How Do You Use Cython to Speed Up Python Code by Compiling It to C?

What is Cython?

Cython is a superset of Python that allows you to compile Python code into C. This can significantly speed up the performance of CPU-bound tasks by taking advantage of C-level optimizations.

Installation:

```
pip install cython
```

Creating a Simple Cython Module:

1. **Create a .pyx file (e.g., example.pyx):**

```
# example.pyx
def sum_numbers(int n):
    cdef int total = 0
    for i in range(n):
        total += i
    return total
```

2. **Create a setup.py file:**

```
from setuptools import setup
```

```
from Cython.Build import cythonize

setup(
    ext_modules = cythonize("example.pyx")
)
```

3. **Compile the Cython Module**:

```
python setup.py build_ext --inplace
```

4. **Use the Compiled Module**:

```
import example

# Faster sum calculation
print(example.sum_numbers(1000000))
```

Benefits:

- Up to **10-100x speed improvements** for computation-heavy code.

- Can use **C data types** for further optimizations.

How Do You Leverage Just-In-Time Compilation Using PyPy?

What is PyPy?

PyPy is an alternative Python interpreter that includes a Just-In-Time (JIT) compiler. The JIT compiler dynamically compiles frequently executed parts of the code into machine code, leading to significant performance boosts for certain workloads.

Installation:

```
# Download PyPy from the official website or use the package manager
brew install pypy3  # Example for macOS
```

Using PyPy for Performance:

1. **Run a Python Script with PyPy**:

```
pypy3 script.py
```

2. **Compare Performance**: Run the same script with python and pypy3 to compare execution times, especially for **CPU-bound** code.

Use Cases:

- Suitable for **long-running processes** where JIT can optimize frequently executed code paths.

- Not ideal for short scripts due to JIT warm-up time.

How Do You Optimize Python Code for Numerical Computations Using NumPy?

Optimizing with NumPy

NumPy is a fundamental library for numerical computation in Python. It is highly optimized for **vectorized operations** using low-level C and Fortran libraries.

Examples of Optimization:

1. **Avoid Loops - Use Vectorized Operations**:

```python
import numpy as np

# Avoid using a Loop
data = np.arange(1000000)
result = data * 2  # Vectorized operation (faster)
```

2. **Use numpy Functions**: Functions provided by numpy are generally faster than custom Python implementations:

```python
# Sum using NumPy (faster)
total = np.sum(data)
```

3. **Memory Efficiency**: Use appropriate data types (float32 instead of float64) to reduce memory consumption:

```python
data = np.array([1, 2, 3, 4], dtype=np.float32)
```

Benefits:

- Significantly **faster computations** than native Python loops.

- Lower **memory usage** due to compact data storage.

How Do You Use Asynchronous Programming to Improve the Performance of I/O-Bound Applications?

What is Asynchronous Programming?

Asynchronous programming allows you to perform non-blocking operations, making it ideal for I/O-bound tasks such as file handling, network requests, or database operations.

Example - Using asyncio for Asynchronous I/O:

```python
import asyncio

# Asynchronous function for I/O-bound task
async def fetch_data(url):
    print(f"Fetching data from {url}...")
    await asyncio.sleep(2)  # Simulating network I/O delay
    return f"Data from {url}"

# Main async function
async def main():
    urls = ['http://example1.com', 'http://example2.com']
    tasks = [fetch_data(url) for url in urls]
    results = await asyncio.gather(*tasks)
    print(results)

# Run the main async function
asyncio.run(main())
```

Benefits:

- **Non-blocking** operations keep the program responsive.

- Efficient handling of **multiple simultaneous I/O tasks**.

How Do You Benchmark Code Performance Using the timeit Module?

What is timeit?

The timeit module is a Python tool for measuring the execution time of small code snippets, helping you compare different implementations and optimize performance.

Basic Usage of timeit:

1. **Measure a Single Statement:**

```python
import timeit
# Benchmarking a simple loop
execution_time = timeit.timeit('sum([x for x in range(1000)])',
number=1000)
print(f"Execution time: {execution_time} seconds")
```

2. **Benchmark a Function:**

```python
def compute_sum():
    return sum(x for x in range(1000))
# Benchmark the function
execution_time = timeit.timeit(compute_sum, number=1000)
print(f"Execution time: {execution_time} seconds")
```

3. **Using Command Line:** You can also run timeit from the command line:

```
python -m timeit -s "from math import sqrt" "sqrt(144)"
```

Tips for Using timeit:

- Use number to specify how many times to run the snippet.

- Use repeat for multiple runs to get a better average.

- Prefer using timeit over manual timing with time for small snippets due to reduced interference.

3.5 Security Best Practices in Python

How Do You Handle User Input Safely to Prevent Injection Attacks (e.g., SQL Injection, XSS)?

User input is a primary source of security vulnerabilities, including SQL Injection and Cross-Site Scripting (XSS). Proper validation and sanitation of user input are crucial.

SQL Injection Prevention

SQL Injection occurs when user input is directly inserted into a SQL query, allowing attackers to execute malicious SQL code.

Safe Practices:

- Use **parameterized queries** instead of formatting SQL directly.

- Use **ORMs (Object-Relational Mappers)** like SQLAlchemy or Django ORM, which handle SQL safely.

Example - Parameterized Query with sqlite3:

```python
import sqlite3

# Unsafe way (vulnerable to SQL Injection)
user_input = "some_input'; DROP TABLE users; --"
query = f"SELECT * FROM users WHERE username = '{user_input}'"
cursor.execute(query)  # Never do this!
# Safe way using parameterized queries
query = "SELECT * FROM users WHERE username = ?"
cursor.execute(query, (user_input,))  # Safe and secure
```

XSS Prevention

Cross-Site Scripting (XSS) occurs when user input is rendered without escaping, allowing the execution of malicious scripts.

Safe Practices:

- Always **escape output** when rendering user input in templates.

- Use templating engines like **Jinja2**, which automatically escape output.

Example - Safe Output in Jinja2:

```html
<!-- Safe way in Jinja2 (auto-escapes output) -->
<p>{{ user_input }}</p>
```

How Do You Encrypt and Decrypt Sensitive Data Using Python's cryptography Module?

Sensitive data, such as passwords or personal information, should be encrypted before storage or transmission. The cryptography module provides a secure way to handle encryption.

Installation:

```
pip install cryptography
```

Example - Encrypting and Decrypting Data:

```python
from cryptography.fernet import Fernet

# Generate and save a key
key = Fernet.generate_key()
cipher = Fernet(key)

# Encrypt data
plaintext = b"Sensitive information"
encrypted = cipher.encrypt(plaintext)
print(f"Encrypted: {encrypted}")

# Decrypt data
decrypted = cipher.decrypt(encrypted)
print(f"Decrypted: {decrypted.decode()}")
```

Best Practices:

- **Never hard-code encryption keys**; store them securely (e.g., environment variables or vaults).

- Use **Fernet** for symmetric encryption (secret key), which ensures data integrity.

How Do You Implement Secure Password Hashing in Python Using bcrypt or argon2?

Passwords should never be stored as plain text. Instead, they should be securely hashed using algorithms like bcrypt or argon2, which provide resistance to brute-force attacks.

Installation:

```
pip install bcrypt argon2-cffi
```

Example - Using bcrypt for Password Hashing:

```python
import bcrypt

# Hash a password
password = b"super_secret_password"
hashed = bcrypt.hashpw(password, bcrypt.gensalt())
print(f"Hashed Password: {hashed}")

# Verify password
if bcrypt.checkpw(password, hashed):
    print("Password is correct!")
else:
    print("Password is incorrect.")
```

Example - Using argon2 for Password Hashing:

```python
from argon2 import PasswordHasher

ph = PasswordHasher()

# Hash a password
hashed = ph.hash("super_secret_password")
print(f"Hashed Password: {hashed}")

# Verify password
try:
    ph.verify(hashed, "super_secret_password")
    print("Password is correct!")
except Exception:
    print("Password is incorrect.")
```

Best Practices:

- Use **salted hashes** to make each password unique.

- Choose a strong hashing algorithm like argon2 for better security.

How Do You Prevent Cross-Site Request Forgery (CSRF) in Django or Flask?

Cross-Site Request Forgery (CSRF) is an attack that tricks a user into executing unwanted actions on a web application where they're authenticated.

Preventing CSRF in Django:

Django has built-in CSRF protection:

- **Enable CSRF middleware** (default in Django).

- Use {% csrf_token %} in HTML forms.

Example - CSRF Token in Django:

```html
<form method="POST">
    {% csrf_token %}
    <input type="text" name="data">
    <button type="submit">Submit</button>
</form>
```

Preventing CSRF in Flask:

In Flask, you can use **Flask-WTF**, which provides CSRF protection out-of-the-box.

Example - CSRF Protection in Flask:

1. **Installation**:

   ```
   pip install Flask-WTF
   ```

2. **Usage**:

   ```python
   from flask import Flask, render_template
   from flask_wtf import FlaskForm
   from wtforms import StringField, SubmitField
   from flask_wtf.csrf import CSRFProtect

   app = Flask(__name__)
   app.config['SECRET_KEY'] = 'your_secret_key'
   csrf = CSRFProtect(app)

   class MyForm(FlaskForm):
       name = StringField('Name')
       submit = SubmitField('Submit')

   @app.route('/form', methods=['GET', 'POST'])
   def form():
   ```

```
    form = MyForm()
    if form.validate_on_submit():
        return 'Form submitted!'
    return render_template('form.html', form=form)
```

How Do You Secure API Endpoints Using JSON Web Tokens (JWT)?

JWT (JSON Web Tokens) are a standard for securely transmitting information between a client and a server. JWTs can be used for API authentication.

Installation:

```
pip install PyJWT
```

Example - Creating and Verifying JWTs:

```python
import jwt
import datetime

# Secret key for signing the token
secret_key = "your_secret_key"

# Create a JWT
payload = {
    "user_id": 123,
    "exp": datetime.datetime.utcnow() + datetime.timedelta(hours=1)  # Expiration time
}
token = jwt.encode(payload, secret_key, algorithm="HS256")
print(f"Generated Token: {token}")

# Verify and decode the JWT
try:
    decoded = jwt.decode(token, secret_key, algorithms=["HS256"])
    print(f"Decoded Payload: {decoded}")
except jwt.ExpiredSignatureError:
    print("Token has expired.")
except jwt.InvalidTokenError:
    print("Invalid token.")
```

Best Practices:

- Use **short expiration times** for tokens.

- Securely store the **secret key**.

- Implement **refresh tokens** for long-term sessions.

What Are Common Security Vulnerabilities in Python Applications, and How Do You Mitigate Them?

Common Vulnerabilities:

1. **SQL Injection**: Mitigate with parameterized queries or ORM.

2. **Cross-Site Scripting (XSS)**: Sanitize user inputs and escape output.

3. **Insecure Deserialization**: Avoid using pickle with untrusted data. Use safer serialization formats like **JSON**.

4. **Improper Error Handling**: Avoid exposing sensitive information in error messages.

5. **Insecure Dependencies**: Regularly update dependencies and check for vulnerabilities.

Mitigation Techniques:

- **Input validation**: Always validate and sanitize user inputs.

- **Security headers**: Implement security headers (e.g., Content-Security-Policy, X-Content-Type-Options).

- **Dependency management**: Use tools like pip-audit to check for vulnerable dependencies.

Example - Using pip-audit:

```
pip install pip-audit
pip-audit  # Scan for vulnerable dependencies
```

How Do You Manage and Secure Sensitive Environment Variables in Python Applications?

Sensitive information, like API keys and database credentials, should not be hard-coded. Use **environment variables** and manage them securely.

Using dotenv to Manage Environment Variables:

1. **Installation**:

   ```
   pip install python-dotenv
   ```

2. **Create a .env File**:

   ```
   SECRET_KEY=your_secret_key
   DATABASE_URL=your_database_url
   ```

3. **Load Environment Variables in Python**:

   ```python
   from dotenv import load_dotenv
   import os

   # Load variables from .env
   load_dotenv()

   # Access environment variables
   secret_key = os.getenv('SECRET_KEY')
   database_url = os.getenv('DATABASE_URL')
   ```

Best Practices:

- Never commit .env files to version control; add them to .gitignore.

- Use **vaults** (like AWS Secrets Manager or HashiCorp Vault) for production secrets.

- Set **strict permissions** for files storing sensitive information.

3.6 Distributed Systems and Microservices

How Do You Build a Microservices Architecture Using Flask or Django?

Overview of Microservices Architecture

Microservices architecture involves breaking down an application into a collection of smaller, loosely coupled services that can be developed, deployed, and scaled independently. Each microservice handles a specific functionality and communicates with others using APIs.

Building Microservices with Flask

Flask is a lightweight web framework ideal for building microservices because of its simplicity and flexibility.

Example - Simple Flask Microservice:

```python
from flask import Flask, jsonify, request

app = Flask(__name__)

# Sample data for a microservice
items = [
    {"id": 1, "name": "Item 1"},
    {"id": 2, "name": "Item 2"}
]

@app.route('/items', methods=['GET'])
def get_items():
    return jsonify(items)

@app.route('/items/<int:item_id>', methods=['GET'])
def get_item(item_id):
    item = next((item for item in items if item['id'] == item_id), None)
    return jsonify(item) if item else ('Item not found', 404)

# Running the microservice
if __name__ == '__main__':
    app.run(port=5000)
```

Building Microservices with Django

Django is a more feature-rich framework suitable for complex services that require built-in functionality like ORM, authentication, and admin interfaces. For microservices, Django's **Django REST Framework (DRF)** is commonly used.

Example - Simple Django Microservice Setup:

1. **Create a Django project** and install Django REST Framework:

```
django-admin startproject microservice
cd microservice
```

```
pip install djangorestframework
```

2. **Create a Django app** and configure REST API:

```
python manage.py startapp items
```

3. **Configure urls.py** to handle API endpoints:

```python
# microservice/urls.py
from django.urls import path, include

urlpatterns = [
    path('api/', include('items.urls')),
]
```

4. **Implement API views in the items app**:

```python
# items/views.py
from rest_framework.response import Response
from rest_framework.decorators import api_view

@api_view(['GET'])
def get_items(request):
    items = [{"id": 1, "name": "Item 1"}, {"id": 2, "name": "Item
2"}]
    return Response(items)
```

How Do You Use Message Queues (e.g., RabbitMQ, Kafka) for Inter-Service Communication in Python?

Message queues facilitate communication between microservices by allowing them to send and receive messages asynchronously. **RabbitMQ** and **Kafka** are popular choices for message brokers.

Using RabbitMQ with pika Library:

1. **Install pika**:

```
pip install pika
```

2. **Producer Example**:

```python
import pika

connection =
pika.BlockingConnection(pika.ConnectionParameters('localhost'))
channel = connection.channel()

# Declare a queue
channel.queue_declare(queue='task_queue', durable=True)

# Send a message to the queue
message = "Hello, World!"
channel.basic_publish(
    exchange='',
    routing_key='task_queue',
    body=message,
    properties=pika.BasicProperties(
        delivery_mode=2,   # Make the message persistent
    )
)
connection.close()
```

3. **Consumer Example**:

```python
import pika

connection =
pika.BlockingConnection(pika.ConnectionParameters('localhost'))
channel = connection.channel()

# Declare the same queue to receive messages
channel.queue_declare(queue='task_queue', durable=True)

def callback(ch, method, properties, body):
    print(f"Received: {body}")
    ch.basic_ack(delivery_tag=method.delivery_tag)

channel.basic_consume(queue='task_queue',
on_message_callback=callback)
```

```
print('Waiting for messages...')
channel.start_consuming()
```

Using Kafka with kafka-python Library:

1. **Install kafka-python:**

    ```
    pip install kafka-python
    ```

2. **Producer Example:**

    ```
    from kafka import KafkaProducer

    producer = KafkaProducer(bootstrap_servers='localhost:9092')
    producer.send('my_topic', b'Hello, Kafka!')
    producer.close()
    ```

3. **Consumer Example:**

    ```
    from kafka import KafkaConsumer
    consumer = KafkaConsumer('my_topic',
    bootstrap_servers='localhost:9092')
    for message in consumer:
        print(f"Received: {message.value.decode()}")
    ```

How Do You Handle Service Discovery and Load Balancing in Distributed Systems?

Service discovery is crucial in distributed systems for locating services dynamically. Load balancing ensures traffic is evenly distributed across services.

Service Discovery with Consul

Consul is a popular tool for service discovery.

1. **Register Services**: Services register themselves with Consul, providing a health check endpoint.

2. **Discover Services**: Clients query Consul to find healthy services.

3. **Load Balancing**: Tools like **HAProxy** or **Nginx** can use Consul to balance requests.

Load Balancing with Nginx

Use **Nginx** as a reverse proxy to load balance between multiple service instances.

Example - Nginx Load Balancer Configuration:

```
http {
    upstream my_service {
        server service1.example.com;
        server service2.example.com;
    }

    server {
        listen 80;
        location / {
            proxy_pass http://my_service;
        }
    }
}
```

Service Discovery in Kubernetes

Kubernetes uses its **internal DNS** for service discovery and **load balancing** is built-in via services of type LoadBalancer.

How Do You Use Celery for Distributed Task Queuing and Scheduling in Python?

Celery is a distributed task queue for handling asynchronous and scheduled tasks. It uses message brokers like **RabbitMQ** or **Redis** to manage tasks.

Installation:

```
pip install celery
pip install redis  # Example for using Redis as a broker
```

Setting Up a Celery Worker:

1. **Create a Celery app**:

   ```
   # tasks.py
   from celery import Celery
   ```

```python
# Create a Celery app
app = Celery('tasks', broker='redis://localhost:6379/0')

@app.task
def add(x, y):
    return x + y
```

2. **Run the Celery worker**:

```
celery -A tasks worker --loglevel=info
```

3. **Sending Tasks**:

```python
from tasks import add

# Sending a task
result = add.delay(4, 6)
print(result.get())  # Output: 10
```

How Do You Implement Resilience and Fault Tolerance in Python Microservices?

Building resilient services is crucial to handle failures gracefully. Here are common practices:

Circuit Breaker Pattern

Prevent a service from repeatedly calling a failed dependency. Use libraries like **pybreaker**.

Example - Using pybreaker:

```python
pip install pybreaker

import pybreaker
# Create a circuit breaker
circuit_breaker = pybreaker.CircuitBreaker(fail_max=3, reset_timeout=60)
@circuit_breaker
def fetch_data():
    # Simulate a service call
    raise Exception("Service not available")
```

Retry Mechanism

Implement retries with backoff using libraries like **tenacity**.

Example - Using tenacity:

```
pip install tenacity

from tenacity import retry, stop_after_attempt, wait_fixed

@retry(stop=stop_after_attempt(3), wait=wait_fixed(2))
def call_service():
    # Simulate a service call
    raise Exception("Temporary failure")

try:
    call_service()
except Exception as e:
    print(f"Service call failed: {e}")
```

How Do You Use Docker to Containerize and Deploy Python Applications?

Docker allows you to package Python applications with their dependencies, ensuring consistent behavior across environments.

Creating a Dockerfile:

```
# Use a base image
FROM python:3.9-slim
# Set the working directory
WORKDIR /app
# Copy the current directory contents into the container
COPY . /app
# Install dependencies
RUN pip install --no-cache-dir -r requirements.txt
# Expose the port the app runs on
EXPOSE 5000
# Command to run the app
CMD ["python", "app.py"]
```

Building and Running the Docker Container:

1. **Build the Docker Image**:

```
docker build -t my_python_app .
```

2. **Run the Docker Container**:

```
docker run -d -p 5000:5000 my_python_app
```

How Do You Use Kubernetes to Orchestrate Python Microservices in a Cloud Environment?

Kubernetes (K8s) is a container orchestration platform that automates the deployment, scaling, and management of containerized applications.

Deploying a Python App in Kubernetes:

1. **Create a Deployment Configuration** (deployment.yaml):

```yaml
apiVersion: apps/v1
kind: Deployment
metadata:
  name: python-app
spec:
  replicas: 3
  selector:
    matchLabels:
      app: python-app
  template:
    metadata:
      labels:
        app: python-app
    spec:
      containers:
      - name: python-container
        image: my_python_app:latest
        ports:
        - containerPort: 5000
```

2. **Deploy to Kubernetes**:

```
kubectl apply -f deployment.yaml
```

3. **Expose the Service** (service.yaml):

```
apiVersion: v1
kind: Service
metadata:
  name: python-service
spec:
  type: LoadBalancer
  selector:
    app: python-app
  ports:
  - protocol: TCP
    port: 80
    targetPort: 5000
```

4. **Deploy the Service**:

```
kubectl apply -f service.yaml
```

Key Features:

- **Scaling**: Easily scale your microservices with kubectl scale.

- **Load Balancing**: Kubernetes automatically handles load balancing across replicas.

- **Service Discovery**: Kubernetes provides built-in DNS for discovering services within the cluster.

3.7 Working with Big Data in Python

How Do You Work With PySpark for Big Data Processing in Python?

PySpark is the Python API for Apache Spark, a framework that enables large-scale data processing across distributed computing clusters. PySpark can handle big data efficiently through parallel processing and offers tools for machine learning and data transformations.

220

Setting Up PySpark

To use PySpark, you need a **SparkSession**, which acts as the main entry point for interacting with Spark.

Example - Basic Data Processing with PySpark:

```python
from pyspark.sql import SparkSession

# Create a Spark session
spark = SparkSession.builder.appName("BigDataExample").getOrCreate()

# Load data from a CSV file
df = spark.read.csv("large_data.csv", header=True, inferSchema=True)

# Filter data and perform aggregations
df_filtered = df.filter(df['age'] > 30)
df_grouped = df_filtered.groupBy("department").count()

# Display results
df_grouped.show()

# Stop the Spark session
spark.stop()
```

Key Features:

- **Resilient Distributed Dataset (RDD)**: Core data structure for distributed data processing.

- **DataFrame API**: Optimized for structured data, with SQL-like syntax.

- **MLlib**: A machine learning library for scalable ML algorithms.

Optimization Tips:

- **Partitioning**: Control data partitioning for optimal load distribution using repartition().

- **Caching**: Cache frequently accessed data using df.cache() to avoid recomputation.

How Do You Use Dask for Distributed Data Processing in Python?

Dask is a parallel computing library that extends familiar data structures like **DataFrames** and **arrays** to handle larger-than-memory datasets. It splits computations into tasks and distributes them across multiple cores or nodes.

221

Setting Up Dask

1. **Install Dask**:

```
pip install dask[complete]
```

2. **Process Large Datasets with Dask DataFrames**:

```python
import dask.dataframe as dd
# Load a large dataset as a Dask DataFrame
df = dd.read_csv("large_data.csv")

# Perform transformations
df_filtered = df[df['age'] > 30]
df_grouped = df_filtered.groupby("department").count().compute()
# `compute()` triggers execution

print(df_grouped)
```

Key Features:

- **Dask DataFrames**: Similar to pandas but supports parallel operations and larger-than-memory data.

- **Dask Arrays**: Extends numpy for handling large numerical arrays.

- **Customizable Scheduler**: The Dask scheduler manages task dependencies and parallel execution.

Optimization Tips:

- **Optimize Chunk Size**: Set an optimal chunk size that balances memory usage and processing time.

- **Use In-Place Operations**: Avoid unnecessary copies to reduce memory usage.

How Do You Handle Large Datasets Efficiently Using pandas and NumPy?

When using **pandas** and **NumPy** with large datasets, memory management and processing efficiency are essential.

1. **Using Chunks in pandas:**

   Using the chunksize parameter allows you to load data in small, manageable pieces.

```
import pandas as pd

# Load Large CSV in chunks
chunks = pd.read_csv("large_data.csv", chunksize=10000)
for chunk in chunks:
    processed_chunk = chunk[chunk['value'] > 100]  # Process each
chunk
    # Save or further process the chunk
```

2. **Optimize Data Types in pandas:**

Reducing data types minimizes memory usage, especially for integer and float columns.

```
# Read with specified data types to save memory
df = pd.read_csv("large_data.csv", dtype={'age': 'int8', 'salary':
'float32'})
```

3. **Use Memory-Efficient Arrays in NumPy:**

Use specific data types to reduce memory overhead when creating arrays.

```
import numpy as np

# Create an array with int8 data type
data = np.array([1, 2, 3], dtype=np.int8)
```

Optimization Tips:

- **Avoid Copies**: Use in-place operations (df.sort_values(inplace=True)) to reduce memory overhead.

- **Leverage NumPy for Computations**: Use NumPy for vectorized operations, which are faster and more memory-efficient than iterative processing in pandas.

How Do You Interface Python With Hadoop Ecosystem Tools (e.g., HDFS, Hive)?

Python can interact with the Hadoop ecosystem, including HDFS (Hadoop Distributed File System) and Hive, to work with distributed storage and querying.

Using HDFS with Python:

1. **Install hdfs** for interacting with HDFS:

```
pip install hdfs
```

2. **Read and Write Files to HDFS**:

```python
from hdfs import InsecureClient

# Connect to HDFS
client = InsecureClient('http://localhost:50070', user='hadoop')

# Write data to HDFS
with client.write('/path/to/hdfs/file.csv') as writer:
    writer.write("Hello, HDFS!")

# Read data from HDFS
with client.read('/path/to/hdfs/file.csv') as reader:
    print(reader.read())
```

Using Hive with PyHive:

1. **Install pyhive** for querying Hive databases:

```
pip install pyhive
```

2. **Query Hive Tables**:

```python
from pyhive import hive

conn = hive.Connection(host='localhost', port=10000,
username='hadoop')
cursor = conn.cursor()
cursor.execute('SELECT * FROM my_table LIMIT 10')
for row in cursor.fetchall():
    print(row)
```

Optimization Tips:

- **Leverage Hive Partitioning**: Use partitioned tables in Hive for faster queries on large datasets.

- **Compression**: Store data in compressed formats (e.g., Parquet) for efficient storage and faster I/O.

How Do You Optimize Memory Usage When Processing Big Data in Python?

Optimizing memory usage is crucial for big data applications to avoid crashes and improve performance.

1. **Using Generators Instead of Lists:**

   Generators yield items on demand, reducing memory usage significantly.

   ```python
   # Generator function for large data
   def data_generator():
       for i in range(1000000):
           yield i * i

   for value in data_generator():
       print(value)
   ```

2. **Use Smaller Data Types in pandas and NumPy:**

   Specify data types that require less memory when working with large datasets.

   ```python
   import pandas as pd
   import numpy as np

   # Optimize data types in pandas
   df = pd.read_csv("large_data.csv", dtype={'column1': 'int32',
   'column2': 'float32'})

   # Use int8 in NumPy to save memory
   array = np.array([1, 2, 3], dtype=np.int8)
   ```

3. **Avoid Duplicating Data in Memory:**

   Use in-place operations to reduce memory usage.

   ```python
   # Sort data in-place
   df.sort_values('column1', inplace=True)
   ```

Optimization Tips:

- **Batch Processing**: Process data in small batches to manage memory usage.

- **Use Compression**: Compress large files to save storage and speed up read/write operations.

How Do You Process Streaming Data in Real-Time Using Python (e.g., Kafka, Stream Processing)?

Real-time data streaming involves processing data continuously as it is generated. **Apache Kafka** is commonly used for data streams, and Python can interface with Kafka to consume and produce messages.

Using Kafka with kafka-python:

1. **Install the Library**:

```
pip install kafka-python
```

2. **Producer Example**:

```
from kafka import KafkaProducer

producer = KafkaProducer(bootstrap_servers='localhost:9092')
producer.send('my_topic', b'Streaming data')
producer.close()
```

3. **Consumer Example**:

```
from kafka import KafkaConsumer

consumer = KafkaConsumer('my_topic',
bootstrap_servers='localhost:9092')
for message in consumer:
    print(f"Received: {message.value.decode()}")
```

Stream Processing with PySpark Structured Streaming:

Use PySpark's structured streaming for real-time data processing.

```
from pyspark.sql import SparkSession
spark = SparkSession.builder.appName("StreamProcessing").getOrCreate()
df = spark.readStream.format("kafka").option("kafka.bootstrap.servers",
"localhost:9092")\
    .option("subscribe", "my_topic").load()
df.selectExpr("CAST(value AS
STRING)").writeStream.format("console").start().awaitTermination()
```

Optimization Tips:

- **Windowed Aggregations**: Use time-based windowing to batch events and reduce load.

- **Backpressure Handling**: Configure consumer settings to handle peak loads without dropping data.

How Do You Use Python for ETL (Extract, Transform, Load) Workflows?

ETL workflows involve **Extracting**, **Transforming**, and **Loading** data. Python provides multiple tools and libraries for ETL, such as **pandas** for data manipulation, **SQLAlchemy** for database interactions, and **Airflow** for orchestration.

1. **Extract Data:**

   Extract data from sources like APIs or databases.

   ```python
   import pandas as pd
   import requests

   # Extract data from an API
   response = requests.get("https://api.example.com/data")
   data = response.json()
   df = pd.DataFrame(data)
   ```

2. **Transform Data:**

   Clean and transform data to match target requirements.

   ```python
   # Filter and rename columns
   df = df[df['age'] > 25]
   df.rename(columns={'name': 'full_name'}, inplace=True)
   ```

3. **Load Data:**

   Load transformed data into a target database.

   ```python
   from sqlalchemy import create_engine

   # Database connection
   engine = create_engine('sqlite:///my_database.db')
   df.to_sql('table_name', con=engine, if_exists='replace',
   index=False)
   ```

Using Airflow for ETL Orchestration:

Airflow can automate and schedule ETL pipelines with task dependencies.

```python
from airflow import DAG
from airflow.operators.python_operator import PythonOperator
from datetime import datetime

def extract():
    # Extraction logic here
    pass

def transform():
    # Transformation logic here
    pass
def load():
    # Load data to target

dag = DAG('etl_workflow', start_date=datetime(2023, 1, 1),
schedule_interval='@daily')

extract_task = PythonOperator(task_id='extract',
python_callable=extract, dag=dag)
transform_task = PythonOperator(task_id='transform',
python_callable=transform, dag=dag)
load_task = PythonOperator(task_id='load', python_callable=load,
dag=dag)

extract_task >> transform_task >> load_task  # Set task dependencies
```

Optimization Tips:

- **Parallelize ETL Steps**: Use Airflow to parallelize tasks when possible.

- **Use Bulk Loading**: For large datasets, use bulk operations to load data efficiently.

3.8 Machine Learning and AI in Python

How Do You Use scikit-learn for Machine Learning Model Building?

scikit-learn is a widely used library in Python for building and evaluating machine learning models. It provides modules for classification, regression, clustering, and preprocessing.

Example - Building a Classification Model with scikit-learn:

```python
from sklearn.model_selection import train_test_split
from sklearn.ensemble import RandomForestClassifier
from sklearn.metrics import accuracy_score
from sklearn.datasets import load_iris

# Load a dataset
data = load_iris()
X = data.data
y = data.target
# Split the data
X_train, X_test, y_train, y_test = train_test_split(X, y, test_size=0.3,
random_state=42)

# Initialize and train the model
model = RandomForestClassifier()
model.fit(X_train, y_train)

# Make predictions
y_pred = model.predict(X_test)

# Evaluate the model
accuracy = accuracy_score(y_test, y_pred)
print(f"Accuracy: {accuracy:.2f}")
```

Key Features of scikit-learn:

- **Standardized API**: Consistent methods for model training (fit), prediction (predict), and evaluation.

- **Preprocessing Tools**: Data normalization, scaling, and encoding.

- **Comprehensive Model Library**: Algorithms for both supervised and unsupervised learning.

How Do You Perform Feature Engineering Using pandas and NumPy?

Feature engineering involves creating, modifying, or selecting features to improve model performance. **pandas** and **NumPy** are effective libraries for manipulating and preparing data.

1. **Creating New Features:**

   Use pandas to create features based on existing data.

   ```python
   import pandas as pd
   # Create new features
   df = pd.DataFrame({
       'age': [25, 32, 47, 51],
       'income': [50000, 60000, 120000, 140000]
   })
   # Add a feature based on income per year of age
   df['income_per_age'] = df['income'] / df['age']
   print(df)
   ```

2. **Encoding Categorical Variables:**

   Convert categorical variables into numerical formats using one-hot encoding.

   ```python
   df['gender'] = ['Male', 'Female', 'Female', 'Male']
   df = pd.get_dummies(df, columns=['gender'], drop_first=True)  # Avoids multicollinearity
   print(df)
   ```

3. **Scaling and Normalizing Features:**

   Use StandardScaler from scikit-learn to scale numerical features.

   ```python
   from sklearn.preprocessing import StandardScaler
   scaler = StandardScaler()
   # Scale numeric columns
   df[['age', 'income', 'income_per_age']] = scaler.fit_transform(df[['age', 'income', 'income_per_age']])
   print(df)
   ```

Best Practices:

- **Feature Selection**: Use correlation analysis to remove redundant features.

- **Log Transformations**: For skewed data, apply logarithmic transformations to normalize distributions.

How Do You Train and Test Machine Learning Models Using Cross-Validation?

Cross-validation is a technique for assessing model performance on different subsets of data, helping to reduce overfitting and improve generalization.

Example - k-Fold Cross-Validation with scikit-learn:

```python
from sklearn.model_selection import cross_val_score
from sklearn.ensemble import RandomForestClassifier
from sklearn.datasets import load_iris

# Load dataset
data = load_iris()
X, y = data.data, data.target

# Initialize model
model = RandomForestClassifier()

# Perform 5-fold cross-validation
scores = cross_val_score(model, X, y, cv=5)
print(f"Cross-validation scores: {scores}")
print(f"Average score: {scores.mean():.2f}")
```

Types of Cross-Validation:

- **k-Fold Cross-Validation**: Splits data into k subsets, training on k-1 and testing on the remaining.

- **Stratified k-Fold**: Ensures each fold has a similar distribution of class labels, useful for imbalanced datasets.

How Do You Use TensorFlow and Keras for Deep Learning Models in Python?

TensorFlow and **Keras** are popular frameworks for building deep learning models. Keras provides a high-level API for easy model construction, which runs on top of TensorFlow.

231

Example - Building a Neural Network with Keras:

```python
import tensorflow as tf
from tensorflow.keras.models import Sequential
from tensorflow.keras.layers import Dense
from tensorflow.keras.datasets import mnist

# Load dataset
(X_train, y_train), (X_test, y_test) = mnist.load_data()
X_train, X_test = X_train.reshape(-1, 784) / 255.0, X_test.reshape(-1,
784) / 255.0  # Flatten and normalize

# Define the model
model = Sequential([
    Dense(128, activation='relu', input_shape=(784,)),
    Dense(64, activation='relu'),
    Dense(10, activation='softmax')  # Output layer for classification
])

# Compile the model
model.compile(optimizer='adam', loss='sparse_categorical_crossentropy',
metrics=['accuracy'])

# Train the model
model.fit(X_train, y_train, epochs=5, validation_data=(X_test, y_test))
```

Key Features:

- **Sequential and Functional APIs**: Flexibility to build both simple and complex networks.

- **Integration with TensorFlow**: Leverages TensorFlow's powerful backend for efficient training.

Optimization Tips:

- **Batch Normalization**: Stabilizes and speeds up training.

- **Dropout**: Reduces overfitting by randomly dropping units during training.

How Do You Optimize Hyperparameters in Machine Learning Models Using Grid Search?

Hyperparameter optimization involves tuning model parameters to improve performance. **Grid Search** exhaustively searches across specified parameter values to find the best combination.

Example - Using GridSearchCV for Hyperparameter Tuning:

```python
from sklearn.model_selection import GridSearchCV
from sklearn.ensemble import RandomForestClassifier
from sklearn.datasets import load_iris

# Load dataset
data = load_iris()
X, y = data.data, data.target

# Define model and parameter grid
model = RandomForestClassifier()
param_grid = {
    'n_estimators': [50, 100, 150],
    'max_depth': [None, 10, 20]
}

# Perform grid search
grid_search = GridSearchCV(model, param_grid, cv=5)
grid_search.fit(X, y)

print(f"Best parameters: {grid_search.best_params_}")
print(f"Best score: {grid_search.best_score_:.2f}")
```

Key Considerations:

- **Grid Search**: Suitable for small parameter grids but computationally expensive for large grids.

- **Randomized Search**: Tests random combinations of parameters, often faster than Grid Search.

How Do You Deploy Machine Learning Models as APIs Using Flask or FastAPI?

Flask and FastAPI are lightweight web frameworks that make it easy to deploy machine learning models as APIs, allowing models to serve predictions to external applications.

Example - Deploying a Model with Flask:

1. **Train and Save the Model:**

```python
from sklearn.ensemble import RandomForestClassifier
import pickle

# Train model
model = RandomForestClassifier()
model.fit(X, y)

# Save the model
with open("model.pkl", "wb") as file:
    pickle.dump(model, file)
```

2. **Create a Flask API:**

```python
from flask import Flask, request, jsonify
import pickle

app = Flask(__name__)

# Load the model
with open("model.pkl", "rb") as file:
    model = pickle.load(file)

@app.route('/predict', methods=['POST'])
def predict():
    data = request.get_json()  # Expect input in JSON format
    prediction = model.predict([data['features']])
    return jsonify({'prediction': int(prediction[0])})

if __name__ == '__main__':
    app.run(port=5000)
```

3. **Test the API:** Send a POST request with JSON input to get predictions.

```
curl -X POST http://localhost:5000/predict -H "Content-Type:
application/json" -d '{"features": [5.1, 3.5, 1.4, 0.2]}'
```

234

Optimization Tips:

- **FastAPI for Asynchronous Processing**: FastAPI supports asynchronous requests, making it faster than Flask for high-throughput applications.

- **Docker**: Containerize the API for consistent deployment across environments.

How Do You Work With Imbalanced Datasets in Machine Learning?

Imbalanced datasets, where one class significantly outnumbers others, can lead to biased models. Techniques like **resampling** and **algorithmic adjustments** are used to handle these issues.

1. **Resampling Techniques:**

   - **Oversampling**: Duplicate examples from the minority class.

   - **Undersampling**: Reduce examples from the majority class.

```python
from imblearn.over_sampling import SMOTE
from sklearn.model_selection import train_test_split

# Load dataset
X_train, X_test, y_train, y_test = train_test_split(X, y,
test_size=0.3, random_state=42)

# Apply SMOTE for oversampling
smote = SMOTE(random_state=42)
X_resampled, y_resampled = smote.fit_resample(X_train, y_train)
```

2. **Algorithmic Adjustments:**

   Class Weights: Assign higher weights to minority classes to reduce bias.

```python
from sklearn.ensemble import RandomForestClassifier

# Set class weights
model = RandomForestClassifier(class_weight='balanced')
model.fit(X_train, y_train)
```

Evaluation Metrics:

For imbalanced datasets, metrics like **precision**, **recall**, and **F1-score** are more informative than accuracy.

235

```
from sklearn.metrics import classification_report

y_pred = model.predict(X_test)
print(classification_report(y_test, y_pred))
```

Best Practices:

- **Use Stratified k-Fold Cross-Validation**: Ensures each fold contains a similar distribution of classes.

- **Evaluate with ROC-AUC**: Provides a robust measure for classifier performance on imbalanced data.

3.9 Cloud Computing with Python

How Do You Deploy Python Applications to AWS Lambda for Serverless Architectures?

AWS Lambda enables you to run Python applications without provisioning or managing servers. Lambda functions can be triggered by various AWS services, allowing for fully serverless architecture.

Steps to Deploy a Python Function to AWS Lambda:

1. **Write the Lambda Function:**

   ```
   # lambda_function.py
   def lambda_handler(event, context):
       return {"statusCode": 200, "body": "Hello from Lambda!"}
   ```

2. **Create and Deploy via AWS Console or AWS CLI:**

   Using the AWS Console: Navigate to the Lambda service, create a function, and upload the code or provide it inline.

   Using AWS CLI:

   ```
   aws lambda create-function \
     --function-name myLambdaFunction \
     --runtime python3.8 \
   ```

```
--role arn:aws:iam::YOUR_ACCOUNT_ID:role/your-role \
--handler lambda_function.lambda_handler \
--zip-file fileb://function.zip
```

3. **Trigger Lambda**: Lambda can be triggered by events from S3, DynamoDB, API Gateway, and more.

Optimization Tips:

- **Reduce Package Size**: Minimize deployment package size for faster execution.

- **Environment Variables**: Use Lambda environment variables for sensitive information like API keys.

How Do You Use Boto3 to Manage AWS Resources in Python?

Boto3 is the AWS SDK for Python, allowing you to interact with AWS services such as S3, EC2, and DynamoDB.

Example - Managing S3 Buckets with Boto3:

1. **Install Boto3**:

```
pip install boto3
```

2. **Create a New S3 Bucket**:

```python
import boto3
s3 = boto3.client('s3')
s3.create_bucket(Bucket='my-new-bucket')
```

3. **Upload a File to S3**:

```python
s3.upload_file('local_file.txt', 'my-new-bucket', 'uploaded_file.txt')
```

4. **List All S3 Buckets:**

```python
response = s3.list_buckets()
for bucket in response['Buckets']:
    print(bucket['Name'])
```

Additional Capabilities:

- **EC2 Management**: Start, stop, and monitor EC2 instances.

- **DynamoDB**: Create, query, and manage NoSQL tables.

- **IAM and Security**: Set permissions and manage access.

How Do You Build and Deploy Python Applications Using Docker and AWS EC2?

Docker allows you to package Python applications with dependencies, and EC2 provides scalable compute resources.

Steps for Building and Deploying with Docker and EC2:

1. **Create a Dockerfile**:

```
# Dockerfile
FROM python:3.8-slim
WORKDIR /app
COPY . /app
RUN pip install -r requirements.txt
EXPOSE 5000
CMD ["python", "app.py"]
```

2. **Build and Run Docker Image Locally**:

```
docker build -t my-python-app .
docker run -p 5000:5000 my-python-app
```

3. **Deploy Dockerized Application to EC2**:

Launch an EC2 instance, install Docker, and pull the Docker image from your Docker registry (e.g., Docker Hub or ECR).

Run the Docker container on EC2:

```
docker run -d -p 80:5000 my-python-app
```

Additional Tips:

- **Use EC2 Auto Scaling** for high-availability applications.

- **ECR Integration**: Use Amazon Elastic Container Registry (ECR) to store Docker images securely.

How Do You Automate Cloud Infrastructure Management Using Python and Terraform?

Terraform is a tool for defining and provisioning infrastructure as code (IaC), and Python can automate Terraform workflows.

Steps to Automate with Python and Terraform:

1. **Install Terraform and Python Packages**:

```
brew install terraform
pip install python-terraform
```

2. **Write a Terraform Configuration**:

```
# main.tf
provider "aws" {
  region = "us-east-1"
}

resource "aws_s3_bucket" "my_bucket" {
  bucket = "my-terraform-bucket"
}
```

3. **Run Terraform with Python**:

```
from python_terraform import Terraform
tf = Terraform()
tf.init()
tf.apply(skip_plan=True)  # Applies the configuration
```

Benefits of Terraform:

- **Reusable Infrastructure**: Define configurations once and reuse them across environments.

- **Version Control**: Track infrastructure changes in source control for transparency and collaboration.

How Do You Use Python to Manage Cloud Databases (e.g., Amazon RDS, Google Cloud SQL)?

Python can manage cloud databases through **Boto3** (for Amazon RDS) or **Google Cloud SDK** (for Google Cloud SQL).

Example - Managing Amazon RDS with Boto3:

1. **Launch a New RDS Instance**:

```python
import boto3
rds = boto3.client('rds')
response = rds.create_db_instance(
    DBName='mydatabase',
    DBInstanceIdentifier='mydbinstance',
    MasterUsername='admin',
    MasterUserPassword='password',
    DBInstanceClass='db.t2.micro',
    Engine='mysql',
    AllocatedStorage=20
)
```

2. **Access an RDS Database**: Once created, use standard database connectors, such as mysql-connector-python for MySQL, to connect and perform operations.

Google Cloud SQL:

- Use the **Google Cloud SDK** or **SQLAlchemy** to manage Google Cloud SQL databases.

- Ensure secure access by managing **Cloud IAM roles** and using **private IP** where possible.

How Do You Implement Auto-Scaling for Python Applications on AWS or Google Cloud?

Auto-scaling automatically adjusts the number of running instances based on demand, ensuring efficient resource usage.

Auto-Scaling on AWS:

1. **Set Up Auto Scaling Group in EC2**:

   o Define **Launch Configuration**: Specifies the instance type, AMI, and configurations.

- Create Auto Scaling Group: Choose the minimum, maximum, and desired instance counts and configure scaling policies based on CPU or memory usage.

2. **Configure Scaling Policies**:
   - Scale-out when **CPU utilization** exceeds a certain threshold (e.g., 80%).
   - Scale-in when utilization drops below a certain threshold.

Auto-Scaling on Google Cloud:

Google Compute Engine (GCE) and Google Kubernetes Engine (GKE) offer auto-scaling policies similar to AWS.

- **Instance Groups in GCE**: Set up **managed instance groups** with auto-scaling policies.

- **Kubernetes Horizontal Pod Auto-scaler**: Scales containers in GKE based on CPU, memory, or custom metrics.

How Do You Use gcloud or awscli for Automating Cloud Deployments in Python?

gcloud and awscli provide command-line interfaces for managing Google Cloud and AWS resources. Python's subprocess module can invoke these commands for automation.

Example - Automating with awscli in Python:

```python
import subprocess

# List all S3 buckets using awscli
subprocess.run(["aws", "s3", "ls"])

# Launch an EC2 instance
subprocess.run([
    "aws", "ec2", "run-instances",
    "--image-id", "ami-0abcdef1234567890",
    "--instance-type", "t2.micro",
    "--key-name", "my-key-pair"
])
```

Example - Automating with gcloud in Python:

```python
# Create a GCE instance
```

```
subprocess.run([
    "gcloud", "compute", "instances", "create", "my-instance",
    "--zone=us-central1-a",
    "--machine-type=e2-micro",
    "--image-family=debian-10",
    "--image-project=debian-cloud"
])
```

Best Practices:

- **Script Logging**: Log outputs from subprocesses to help track automation tasks.

- **Error Handling**: Handle errors in subprocess calls for reliable automation.

How Do You Integrate Python Applications With Cloud Storage Services (e.g., AWS S3, Google Cloud Storage)?

Python integrates seamlessly with cloud storage services like AWS S3 and Google Cloud Storage.

Example - Working with AWS S3 Using Boto3:

```
import boto3

s3 = boto3.client('s3')

# Upload a file
s3.upload_file('local_file.txt', 'my-bucket', 'uploaded_file.txt')

# Download a file
s3.download_file('my-bucket', 'uploaded_file.txt',
'downloaded_file.txt')
```

Example - Working with Google Cloud Storage:

1. **Install Google Cloud Storage Client:**

   ```
   pip install google-cloud-storage
   ```

2. **Upload and Download Files:**

   ```
   from google.cloud import storage
   ```

```
client = storage.Client()
bucket = client.get_bucket('my-bucket')

# Upload
blob = bucket.blob('uploaded_file.txt')
blob.upload_from_filename('local_file.txt')

# Download
blob.download_to_filename('downloaded_file.txt')
```

How Do You Implement Continuous Integration and Continuous Deployment (CI/CD) for Python Applications in the Cloud?

CI/CD automates code testing, building, and deployment. Popular CI/CD tools include **GitHub Actions**, **Jenkins**, and **AWS CodePipeline**.

Example - CI/CD with GitHub Actions:

1. **Define a Workflow File** in .github/workflows/main.yml:

```yaml
name: CI/CD Pipeline

on:
  push:
    branches: [main]

jobs:
  build:
    runs-on: ubuntu-latest

    steps:
    - name: Checkout code
      uses: actions/checkout@v2

    - name: Set up Python
      uses: actions/setup-python@v2
      with:
        python-version: '3.8'

    - name: Install dependencies
```

```
        run: |
          pip install -r requirements.txt
          pip install pytest

      - name: Run tests
        run: pytest
```

2. **Automate Deployment**: Configure deployment steps to deploy artifacts to cloud platforms like AWS Elastic Beanstalk or Google App Engine.

Best Practices:

- **Automated Testing**: Run tests on every push to the main branch.

- **Environment Variables**: Store secrets and API keys securely as environment variables in GitHub Actions or Jenkins.

How Do You Use Kubernetes to Orchestrate Dockerized Python Applications in the Cloud?

Kubernetes orchestrates Docker containers, managing deployment, scaling, and load balancing.

Steps for Deploying a Dockerized Python App with Kubernetes:

1. **Create a Kubernetes Deployment Configuration** (deployment.yaml):

```
apiVersion: apps/v1
kind: Deployment
metadata:
  name: python-app
spec:
  replicas: 3
  selector:
    matchLabels:
      app: python-app
  template:
    metadata:
      labels:
        app: python-app
    spec:
      containers:
      - name: python-container
```

```
      image: my-python-app:latest
      ports:
      - containerPort: 5000
```

2. **Deploy to Kubernetes**:

```
kubectl apply -f deployment.yaml
```

3. **Expose the Service** (service.yaml):

```
apiVersion: v1
kind: Service
metadata:
  name: python-service
spec:
  type: LoadBalancer
  selector:
    app: python-app
  ports:
  - protocol: TCP
    port: 80
    targetPort: 5000
```

4. **Apply Service Configuration**:

```
kubectl apply -f service.yaml
```

Best Practices:

- **Auto-scaling**: Configure horizontal pod auto-scaling for load handling.

- **Monitoring**: Use Kubernetes tools like **Prometheus** and **Grafana** for observability.

3.10 DevOps and Automation with Python

How Do You Automate Infrastructure Tasks Using Python With Tools Like Fabric or Ansible?

Fabric and **Ansible** are two popular Python-based tools for automating server and infrastructure tasks.

Fabric

Fabric is a Python library for executing shell commands on remote servers via SSH, making it useful for deploying and managing server configurations.

1. **Install Fabric**:

```
pip install fabric
```

2. **Example - Using Fabric to Restart a Service**:

```python
from fabric import Connection
# Connect to the remote server
conn = Connection("user@hostname")
# Restart a service
conn.run("sudo systemctl restart nginx")
```

3. **Executing Multiple Commands**:

```python
def deploy():
    with Connection("user@hostname") as conn:
        conn.run("git pull origin main")
        conn.run("pip install -r requirements.txt")
        conn.run("sudo systemctl restart app")
```

Ansible

Ansible uses YAML playbooks to automate tasks across multiple servers.

1. **Install Ansible**:

```
sudo apt install ansible
```

2. **Example - Ansible Playbook to Install NGINX**:

```yaml
# install_nginx.yml
- hosts: webservers
  become: true
  tasks:
    - name: Install NGINX
      apt:
        name: nginx
        state: present
```

3. **Run the Playbook**:

```
ansible-playbook -i inventory install_nginx.yml
```

Use Cases:

- **Configuration Management**: Apply consistent configurations across servers.

- **Automated Deployments**: Streamline deployments with Fabric or Ansible playbooks.

How Do You Use Python to Write Bash Scripts for Server Automation?

Python's subprocess module allows you to run shell commands directly from Python, making it ideal for automation scripts that need to interact with the server's shell.

Example - Running Bash Commands with subprocess:

```python
import subprocess
# Run a simple bash command
subprocess.run(["echo", "Hello from Python!"])
# Run multiple commands in sequence
subprocess.run("sudo apt update && sudo apt install -y nginx",
shell=True)
```

Using os.system for Simple Commands:

os.system can also be used, although subprocess is generally preferred for better control.

```python
import os
os.system("ls -la")
```

Automation Script Example:

Create a script that automates updates and service restarts.

```python
import subprocess

def update_and_restart():
    subprocess.run("sudo apt update && sudo apt upgrade -y", shell=True)
    subprocess.run("sudo systemctl restart nginx", shell=True)

update_and_restart()
```

Best Practices:

- **Error Handling**: Use try-except blocks or subprocess.CalledProcessError to handle command failures.

- **Logging**: Log outputs of each command to help diagnose issues during automation.

How Do You Set Up CI/CD Pipelines Using Jenkins or GitLab for Python Projects?

Continuous Integration and Continuous Deployment (CI/CD) pipelines automate the process of testing, building, and deploying applications.

Jenkins Pipeline Setup

1. **Install Jenkins and Plugins**: Install Jenkins, then add plugins like **Git**, **GitHub**, and **Docker** if needed.

2. **Define a Jenkins Pipeline**:

   Create a Jenkinsfile in your project's root directory to define the pipeline steps.

   ```
   pipeline {
       agent any
       stages {
           stage('Build') {
               steps {
                   sh 'pip install -r requirements.txt'
               }
           }
           stage('Test') {
   ```

```
                steps {
                    sh 'pytest tests/'
                }
            }
            stage('Deploy') {
                steps {
                    sh './deploy.sh'
                }
            }
        }
    }
```

3. **Push Code to Trigger Pipeline**: Configure the Jenkins job to trigger on push events or pull requests.

GitLab CI/CD Pipeline Setup

1. **Define a .gitlab-ci.yml File**:

Place this file in the root directory of your GitLab repository.

```
stages:
  - build
  - test
  - deploy

build_job:
  stage: build
  script:
    - pip install -r requirements.txt

test_job:
  stage: test
  script:
    - pytest tests/

deploy_job:
  stage: deploy
  script:
    - ./deploy.sh
```

2. **Run Pipeline on Push**: GitLab automatically triggers the pipeline for each push or pull request.

Best Practices:

- **Automated Testing**: Run unit and integration tests at each stage to catch issues early.

- **Environment Variables**: Use secrets or environment variables for sensitive data.

How Do You Automate Docker Builds and Deployment of Python Applications?

Automating Docker builds and deployments simplifies the CI/CD pipeline and ensures consistent environments.

Automating Docker Builds with Dockerfile:

1. **Write a Dockerfile**:

```
# Dockerfile
FROM python:3.8-slim
WORKDIR /app
COPY . /app
RUN pip install -r requirements.txt
CMD ["python", "app.py"]
```

2. **Build and Push Docker Image Automatically**:

```
docker build -t my-python-app .
docker tag my-python-app:latest my-dockerhub-username/my-python-app:latest
docker push my-dockerhub-username/my-python-app:latest
```

3. **Automate with CI/CD**: Integrate the Docker build and push steps into Jenkins, GitLab, or GitHub Actions for automated deployment on each push.

Deployment to Docker Containers:

1. **Run the Docker Container Locally**:

```
docker run -d -p 5000:5000 my-python-app
```

2. **Deploy to Cloud Platforms**: Use AWS ECS or Google Cloud Run to host Docker containers in production.

How Do You Use Python for Log Aggregation and Monitoring in a DevOps Environment?

Log aggregation and monitoring enable you to collect, analyze, and visualize logs from various servers and services.

Using Log Aggregation Tools (e.g., ELK Stack):

1. **Send Logs to Elasticsearch:**

   Use the **Elasticsearch Python client** to send logs from Python applications to Elasticsearch for aggregation.

   ```python
   from elasticsearch import Elasticsearch

   es = Elasticsearch()
   es.index(index="logs", body={"message": "Application started",
   "level": "INFO"})
   ```

2. **Log Monitoring with ELK Stack:**

   Set up **Elasticsearch, Logstash, and Kibana** to monitor and visualize logs. Logstash collects logs, Elasticsearch indexes them, and Kibana provides dashboards for viewing.

Using Fluentd with Python:

Fluentd can gather logs from Python applications and forward them to logging systems like Elasticsearch.

```python
import logging
from fluent import handler
fluent_handler = handler.FluentHandler('app.log', host='localhost',
port=24224)
logger = logging.getLogger('fluent')
logger.addHandler(fluent_handler)
logger.info({'message': 'Log message', 'level': 'INFO'})
```

Best Practices:

- **Standardize Log Formats**: Use consistent log formats (e.g., JSON) for easy parsing.

- **Centralized Logging**: Aggregate logs from multiple sources for unified monitoring.

How Do You Use psutil to Monitor System Performance Metrics (CPU, Memory, Disk)?

psutil is a Python library for retrieving system performance metrics, such as CPU usage, memory, and disk information.

Installation:

```
pip install psutil
```

Example - Monitoring System Performance:

1. **CPU Usage**:

```python
import psutil

# Get CPU usage in percentage
cpu_usage = psutil.cpu_percent(interval=1)
print(f"CPU Usage: {cpu_usage}%")
```

2. **Memory Usage**:

```python
memory = psutil.virtual_memory()
print(f"Memory Usage: {memory.percent}%")
```

3. **Disk Usage**:

```python
disk = psutil.disk_usage('/')
print(f"Disk Usage: {disk.percent}%")
```

4. **Network Information**:

```python
net_info = psutil.net_io_counters()
print(f"Bytes sent: {net_info.bytes_sent}, Bytes received: {net_info.bytes_recv}")
```

Use Cases:

- **Performance Monitoring**: Integrate psutil data into monitoring dashboards.

- **Resource Alerts**: Trigger alerts when usage exceeds predefined thresholds.

How Do You Use Python for Automating Cloud Infrastructure Provisioning and Configuration?

Python, along with libraries like **Boto3** and **Google Cloud SDK**, can automate the provisioning and configuration of cloud resources.

Using Boto3 for AWS Provisioning:

1. **Create an EC2 Instance**:

```python
import boto3
ec2 = boto3.resource('ec2')
instance = ec2.create_instances(
    ImageId='ami-0abcdef1234567890',
    InstanceType='t2.micro',
    MinCount=1, MaxCount=1
)
print("Instance created with ID:", instance[0].id)
```

2. **Create an S3 Bucket**:

```python
s3 = boto3.client('s3')
s3.create_bucket(Bucket='my-automation-bucket')
```

Using Google Cloud SDK for GCP Provisioning:

1. **Install Google Cloud SDK and Authenticate**:

```
pip install google-cloud-compute
```

2. **Create a GCE Instance**:

```python
from google.cloud import compute_v1
instance_client = compute_v1.InstancesClient()
instance_client.insert(project="my-project", zone="us-central1-a",
instance=instance_config)
```

Benefits:

- **Automated Resource Scaling**: Scale resources up and down based on demand.

- **Automated Provisioning**: Quickly set up multiple cloud resources with predefined configurations.

253

3.11 Advanced Data Processing and Analysis

How Do You Use pandas for Data Analysis and Manipulation in Large Datasets?

pandas is the most popular library for data analysis in Python, providing tools for reading, manipulating, and analyzing datasets. When working with large datasets, several techniques in pandas can optimize performance.

1. **Loading Data in Chunks:**

   Using the chunksize parameter to load data in chunks prevents memory overload.

   ```python
   import pandas as pd

   # Read CSV in chunks
   chunks = pd.read_csv("large_data.csv", chunksize=10000)
   for chunk in chunks:
       # Process each chunk separately
       filtered_chunk = chunk[chunk['column'] > 100]
       # Save or aggregate results from each chunk
   ```

2. **Data Manipulation Techniques:**

   - **Grouping and Aggregation**: Use groupby for efficient aggregation.

   - **Pivot Tables**: Reshape data with pivot_table.

   ```python
   # Example of grouping and aggregating
   df = pd.read_csv("data.csv")
   df_grouped = df.groupby("category").agg({"sales": "sum",
   "quantity": "mean"})
   ```

Optimization Tips:

- **Set data types** during data loading to reduce memory usage.

- **Apply Vectorized Operations**: Avoid loops and use built-in pandas methods for speed.

How Do You Process Large CSV and JSON Files Efficiently in Python?

When working with large files in formats like CSV and JSON, efficient loading and processing are essential.

1. **Use Dask for Parallelized Loading:**

   Dask is a parallel computing library that extends pandas for handling large datasets.

   ```python
   import dask.dataframe as dd

   # Load a large CSV file with Dask
   df = dd.read_csv("large_data.csv")

   # Perform transformations (lazy evaluation)
   df_filtered = df[df['column'] > 100]
   result = df_filtered.compute()  # Compute triggers execution
   ```

2. **Use chunksize in pandas:**

   Pandas allows you to read data in chunks to save memory.

   ```python
   chunks = pd.read_csv("large_data.csv", chunksize=10000)
   for chunk in chunks:
       # Process each chunk here
       pass
   ```

3. **Use JSON Parsing Libraries for Large JSON Files:**

   For JSON, libraries like ijson allow for efficient parsing.

   ```python
   import ijson
   # Stream large JSON data
   with open("large_data.json", "r") as file:
       for item in ijson.items(file, "item"):
           # Process each item in the JSON file
           pass
   ```

Best Practices:

- **Use Compression**: Use compressed file formats (e.g., .csv.gz, .json.gz) to save space.

- **Load Only Necessary Columns**: Limit columns loaded by specifying them during data read.

How Do You Use NumPy for Fast Array Computations and Numerical Operations?

NumPy is essential for numerical computing in Python, providing powerful tools for fast array computations, ideal for handling large datasets.

1. **Basic Array Operations:**

   NumPy's vectorized operations allow for fast computations without explicit loops.

   ```python
   import numpy as np

   # Create arrays
   arr1 = np.array([1, 2, 3])
   arr2 = np.array([4, 5, 6])

   # Perform operations
   result = arr1 + arr2
   ```

2. **Matrix Operations:**

   NumPy provides efficient functions for matrix multiplication, transposition, and inverses.

   ```python
   # Matrix multiplication
   matrix_a = np.array([[1, 2], [3, 4]])
   matrix_b = np.array([[5, 6], [7, 8]])
   result = np.dot(matrix_a, matrix_b)
   ```

3. **Broadcasting:**

   Broadcasting is a technique for applying operations to arrays of different shapes.

   ```python
   arr = np.array([1, 2, 3])
   broadcast_result = arr * 2
   ```

Optimization Tips:

- **Avoid Loops**: Use NumPy's vectorized functions instead of loops for speed.

- **Memory-Efficient Data Types**: Specify data types like float32 instead of float64 when possible to save memory.

How Do You Implement Data Cleaning and Transformation Pipelines in Python?

Data cleaning and transformation pipelines standardize data preparation, making analysis and modeling more efficient.

Using pandas for Cleaning:

1. **Handling Missing Values**:

```python
df['column'].fillna(df['column'].mean(), inplace=True)
```

2. **Removing Outliers**: Use z-score or IQR methods to filter outliers.

```python
from scipy import stats
df = df[(np.abs(stats.zscore(df['column'])) < 3)]
```

Using Custom Transformation Pipelines:

- **Scikit-learn's Pipeline**: Useful for chaining preprocessing steps in ML workflows.

```python
from sklearn.pipeline import Pipeline
from sklearn.preprocessing import StandardScaler
from sklearn.impute import SimpleImputer

pipeline = Pipeline([
    ('imputer', SimpleImputer(strategy='mean')),
    ('scaler', StandardScaler())
])

df_transformed = pipeline.fit_transform(df)
```

Creating Custom Functions for Cleaning:

Create functions for repetitive tasks like renaming columns, encoding, or aggregating.

```python
def clean_data(df):
    df['column'] = df['column'].str.strip().str.lower()
    df.dropna(subset=['important_column'], inplace=True)
    return df

df = clean_data(df)
```

Best Practices:

- **Automation**: Use reusable functions to automate repetitive cleaning tasks.

- **Document Transformations**: Keep notes or documentation on each transformation applied for reproducibility.

How Do You Optimize Memory Usage When Working With Large DataFrames in pandas?

Optimizing memory usage is essential when working with large datasets in pandas.

1. **Set Data Types During Data Load:**

   Specify data types during data loading to minimize memory.

   ```python
   df = pd.read_csv("large_data.csv", dtype={'column': 'int8'})
   ```

2. **Use astype for Data Type Conversion:**

   Convert column data types to more efficient types after loading.

   ```python
   df['column'] = df['column'].astype('float32')
   ```

3. **Drop Unnecessary Columns:**

   Removing unused columns helps reduce memory usage.

   ```python
   df.drop(columns=['unnecessary_column'], inplace=True)
   ```

4. **Process Data in Chunks:**

   For very large files, process data in smaller chunks.

   ```python
   chunks = pd.read_csv("large_data.csv", chunksize=5000)
   for chunk in chunks:
       # Process each chunk
       pass
   ```

Optimization Tips:

- **Use Categoricals**: Convert text columns to categorical types for memory savings.

- **Downcast Numeric Columns**: Use pd.to_numeric() with downcast for integer and float columns.

How Do You Perform Real-Time Data Analytics Using Python (e.g., Stream Processing, Kafka)?

Real-time data analytics enables insights as data is generated. Tools like Kafka, combined with Python, make real-time processing achievable.

Using Kafka for Real-Time Streaming:

1. **Install Kafka and kafka-python Library**:

   ```
   pip install kafka-python
   ```

2. **Produce Messages to Kafka**:

   ```
   from kafka import KafkaProducer

   producer = KafkaProducer(bootstrap_servers='localhost:9092')
   producer.send('my_topic', b'Message content')
   producer.close()
   ```

3. **Consume Messages in Real-Time**:

   ```
   from kafka import KafkaConsumer

   consumer = KafkaConsumer('my_topic',
   bootstrap_servers='localhost:9092')
   for message in consumer:
       print(f"Received message: {message.value.decode()}")
   ```

Using PySpark Structured Streaming:

1. **Set Up Spark Session**:

   ```
   from pyspark.sql import SparkSession
   spark =
   SparkSession.builder.appName("StreamProcessing").getOrCreate()
   ```

2. **Read Data from Kafka**:

   ```
   df =
   spark.readStream.format("kafka").option("kafka.bootstrap.servers",
   ```

```
"localhost:9092").option("subscribe", "my_topic").load()
```

3. **Define Transformations and Write Output**:

```
query =
df.writeStream.outputMode("append").format("console").start()
query.awaitTermination()
```

Best Practices:

- **Windowing**: Use windowing techniques for aggregations over time-based windows.

- **Backpressure**: Manage backpressure in consumers to avoid overloads.

How Do You Use Python for Statistical Analysis and Hypothesis Testing?

Statistical analysis allows for data-driven decision-making, and hypothesis testing evaluates whether findings are statistically significant.

1. **Descriptive Statistics with scipy.stats:**

   Calculate descriptive statistics like mean, median, and standard deviation.

```
import scipy.stats as stats

mean = df['column'].mean()
std_dev = df['column'].std()
```

2. Hypothesis Testing:

   Conduct tests like t-tests, chi-square tests, and ANOVA to test hypotheses.

```
# One-sample t-test
t_stat, p_val = stats.ttest_1samp(df['column'], popmean=0)
print(f"T-statistic: {t_stat}, P-value: {p_val}")
```

3. **Correlation Analysis:**

   Calculate correlations to measure the relationship between variables.

```
correlation = df['column1'].corr(df['column2'])
print(f"Correlation: {correlation}")
```

4. **Linear Regression with** statsmodels:

   Use linear regression to model relationships between variables.

   ```python
   import statsmodels.api as sm

   X = df[['column1', 'column2']]
   y = df['target']
   X = sm.add_constant(X)  # Adds intercept
   model = sm.OLS(y, X).fit()
   print(model.summary())
   ```

Best Practices:

- **Use Correct Test for Data**: Choose tests based on data type and distribution.

- **Interpret P-values Carefully**: A low p-value (e.g., <0.05) indicates statistical significance but does not imply causation.

3.12 Performance Tuning and Optimization

How Do You Use Profiling Tools Like cProfile and line_profiler to Identify Bottlenecks?

Profiling tools help you understand where your code is spending the most time, allowing you to focus optimization efforts on critical sections.

1. **Using cProfile:**

   cProfile is a built-in Python module that provides detailed statistics about function calls, execution time, and call frequency.

   ```python
   import cProfile

   def example_function():
       total = 0
       for i in range(1000000):
           total += i
       return total
   ```

```
# Profile the function
cProfile.run('example_function()')
```

Output Interpretation:

- ncalls: Number of function calls.

- tottime: Time spent in the function itself.

- cumtime: Total time spent in the function and any called functions.

2. **Using line_profiler:**

line_profiler profiles code line by line, providing insights into time spent on each line. Install with:

```
pip install line_profiler
```

- **Define the Function to Profile**:

```python
@profile  # Decorator required by line_profiler
def example_function():
    total = 0
    for i in range(1000000):
        total += i
    return total
```

- **Run line_profiler**:

```
kernprof -l -v example_function.py
```

Use Cases:

- **Identify Slow Code Paths**: Focus on the parts of code that consume the most time.

- **Optimize Line by Line**: Use line_profiler for in-depth analysis of critical functions.

How Do You Improve the Performance of I/O-Bound and CPU-Bound Python Tasks?

For I/O-bound tasks (e.g., file reading, network calls), asynchronous programming is effective, while CPU-bound tasks benefit from parallel processing.

1. **Improve I/O-Bound Tasks Using Asyncio:**

Asynchronous programming enables non-blocking operations, which is ideal for I/O-bound tasks.

```python
import asyncio

async def fetch_data():
    # Simulate I/O operation
    await asyncio.sleep(1)
    return "Data"

async def main():
    data = await fetch_data()
    print(data)

asyncio.run(main())
```

2. **Improve CPU-Bound Tasks Using Multiprocessing:**

CPU-bound tasks can be optimized with the multiprocessing module, which bypasses Python's Global Interpreter Lock (GIL).

```python
from multiprocessing import Pool

def compute_square(n):
    return n * n

with Pool(processes=4) as pool:
    results = pool.map(compute_square, range(1000))
```

Best Practices:

- **Asyncio for I/O-Bound Tasks**: Use asyncio or async libraries like aiohttp for tasks involving I/O.

- **Multiprocessing for CPU-Bound Tasks**: Use multiprocessing for computationally heavy tasks that require CPU resources.

How Do You Use Cython or PyPy to Optimize the Speed of Python Code?

Cython and PyPy can significantly improve Python's performance, especially for code that involves heavy calculations.

1. **Using Cython to Compile Python Code to C:**

   Cython converts Python code into C, which can be compiled for faster execution. Cython is especially effective for numerical computations and loops.

   - **Install Cython**:

   ```
   pip install cython
   ```

   - **Write a Cython File (example.pyx)**:

   ```
   def example_function(int n):
       cdef int i
       cdef int total = 0
       for i in range(n):
           total += i
       return total
   ```

   - **Compile the Cython Code**: Create a setup.py file to build the Cython module.

   ```
   from setuptools import setup
   from Cython.Build import cythonize

   setup(
       ext_modules = cythonize("example.pyx")
   )
   ```

   Run the setup:

   ```
   python setup.py build_ext --inplace
   ```

   - **Use the Compiled Cython Module**:

   ```
   import example
   print(example.example_function(1000000))
   ```

2. **Using PyPy for Just-In-Time (JIT) Compilation:**

PyPy is an alternative Python interpreter with a JIT compiler that speeds up code execution.

1. **Install PyPy**: Follow installation instructions from the PyPy website.

2. **Run Code with PyPy**:

```
pypy my_script.py
```

Use Cases:

- **Cython**: Best for computationally intensive tasks that require direct access to C-level performance.

- **PyPy**: Useful for speeding up general-purpose Python applications without modifying code.

How Do You Improve the Performance of Matrix and Vector Operations Using NumPy?

NumPy is optimized for numerical and matrix operations, making it an excellent choice for performance-critical applications.

1. **Vectorized Operations:**

NumPy operations are vectorized, meaning they operate on whole arrays at once, eliminating loops.

```
import numpy as np
# Vectorized addition
arr1 = np.array([1, 2, 3])
arr2 = np.array([4, 5, 6])
result = arr1 + arr2
```

2. **Use numpy.dot for Matrix Multiplication:**

Matrix multiplication in NumPy is highly optimized.

```
matrix_a = np.array([[1, 2], [3, 4]])
matrix_b = np.array([[5, 6], [7, 8]])
result = np.dot(matrix_a, matrix_b)
```

3. **Broadcasting:**

   Broadcasting applies operations across arrays of different shapes efficiently.

   ```
   arr = np.array([1, 2, 3])
   result = arr * 2  # Broadcasting
   ```

Best Practices:

- **Avoid Loops**: Use vectorized operations to eliminate explicit loops.

- **Use In-Place Operations**: Use in-place operations (e.g., arr += 1) to reduce memory overhead

How Do You Use C Extensions to Speed Up Critical Sections of Python Code?

C Extensions allow you to write performance-critical parts of your Python code in C for maximum speed.

1. **Write a C Function and Use Python's ctypes:**

   - **Write a C File** (example.c):

     ```
     #include <stdio.h>

     int add(int a, int b) {
         return a + b;
     }
     ```

   - **Compile the C File:**

     ```
     gcc -shared -o example.so -fPIC example.c
     ```

   - **Use the C Function in Python:**

     ```
     import ctypes

     # Load the shared library
     example = ctypes.CDLL("./example.so")

     # Call the C function
     result = example.add(5, 3)
     print(result)  # Outputs: 8
     ```

2. **Use Cython for Easier Integration:**

Cython simplifies the process of integrating C code with Python by allowing C code to be written directly in .pyx files.

Use Cases:

- **Numerical Computations**: Great for tasks requiring fast, low-level calculations.

- **High-Frequency Functions**: Ideal for optimizing functions that run frequently or handle large datasets.

How Do You Profile Memory Usage and Identify Leaks Using Tools Like tracemalloc?

Memory profiling is essential for identifying and resolving memory bottlenecks, especially in data-intensive applications.

1. **Using tracemalloc:**

tracemalloc is a built-in Python module that tracks memory allocation.

```
import tracemalloc

tracemalloc.start()

# Code to profile
data = [i for i in range(1000000)]

# Display memory usage
snapshot = tracemalloc.take_snapshot()
top_stats = snapshot.statistics('lineno')

for stat in top_stats[:10]:
    print(stat)
```

2. **Using memory_profiler:**

The memory_profiler library provides line-by-line memory usage statistics.

- **Install memory_profiler:**

```
pip install memory-profiler
```

- **Profile a Function**:

```python
from memory_profiler import profile

@profile
def example_function():
    data = [i for i in range(1000000)]
    return data

example_function()
```

Best Practices:

- **Clear Unused Variables**: Use del to delete unnecessary variables and free memory.

- **Avoid Large Temporary Structures**: Minimize the use of large data structures that are only used temporarily.

What Are the Best Practices for Writing High-Performance Python Code in Data-Intensive Applications?

High-performance Python code focuses on minimizing memory usage, leveraging efficient libraries, and avoiding unnecessary computations.

1. **Use Built-In Data Structures:**

   Python's built-in data structures (e.g., lists, sets, dictionaries) are highly optimized. Use them over custom implementations.

2. **Leverage Efficient Libraries:**

   Use specialized libraries like **NumPy** for numerical operations, **pandas** for data manipulation, and **Dask** for parallel processing.

3. **Optimize Algorithms:**

   Choose algorithms with the best possible complexity for the task. Avoid nested loops or complex calculations in favor of simpler, faster solutions.

4. **Minimize Function Calls:**

   Avoid unnecessary function calls in loops and performance-critical sections, as they add overhead.

5. **Limit Object Creation:**

   Object creation is memory-intensive. Reuse objects when possible, especially in loops.

6. **Use Lazy Evaluation:**

   Generators and iterators are memory efficient and only evaluate when needed.

   ```python
   # Use generator instead of list comprehension
   data = (i for i in range(1000000))
   ```

7. **Profile Code Regularly:**

   Regular profiling helps catch bottlenecks early and ensures efficient use of resources

---

3.13 Distributed Systems and High Scalability

How Do You Design a Scalable Distributed System Using Python?

Designing a scalable distributed system requires careful planning to handle increasing loads while maintaining performance, availability, and reliability. Key principles include microservices, horizontal scaling, and load balancing.

1. **Microservices Architecture:**

   Break the application into loosely coupled services, each responsible for a specific function. This reduces interdependencies, making it easier to scale and maintain each service individually.

   Example: Separate services for authentication, data processing, and logging, each with dedicated resources.

2. **Horizontal Scaling:**

   Horizontal scaling involves adding more servers to handle load, rather than relying on a single, more powerful machine.

   Example: Use container orchestration tools like Kubernetes to spin up additional instances based on demand.

3. **Database Partitioning and Sharding:**

   Divide data across multiple databases or partitions to reduce the load on any single database.

Example: For a user database, you could shard by user ID, so each shard handles a subset of users.

4. **Stateless Services**:

Make services stateless to allow easy scaling. Store user sessions and other stateful data in distributed caches (e.g., Redis).

Best Practices:

- **APIs**: Use REST or gRPC APIs for inter-service communication.

- **Message Queues**: Use a queue (e.g., RabbitMQ, Kafka) for asynchronous processing to decouple services

How Do You Implement Distributed Task Queuing Using Celery or RQ?

Distributed task queues like **Celery** and **RQ** (Redis Queue) enable asynchronous task execution, allowing applications to handle background tasks across multiple workers.

Using Celery:

Celery supports distributed task queues, scheduling, and retry mechanisms.

1. **Install Celery**:

```
pip install celery
```

2. **Set Up Celery with Redis as the Broker**:

```python
from celery import Celery

# Initialize Celery app
app = Celery('tasks', broker='redis://localhost:6379/0')

@app.task
def add(x, y):
    return x + y
```

3. **Run the Worker**:

```
celery -A tasks worker --loglevel=info
```

270

4. **Calling the Task**:

```python
result = add.delay(3, 4)  # Schedules the task in the queue
print(result.get())  # Blocks until the result is ready
```

Using RQ:

RQ (Redis Queue) is a simpler alternative to Celery, primarily focused on Redis as a task queue.

1. **Install RQ**:

```
pip install rq
```

2. **Set Up a Job Queue**:

```python
from rq import Queue
from redis import Redis
from tasks import my_task
redis_conn = Redis()
q = Queue(connection=redis_conn)
q.enqueue(my_task, 3, 4)
```

Use Cases:

- **Background Processing**: Sending emails, processing files, or scheduling jobs.

- **Decoupling Workflows**: Handle tasks asynchronously to prevent blocking critical processes.

How Do You Handle Distributed Locking and Consistency in a Distributed Python Application?

Distributed locking ensures that multiple nodes do not perform the same task simultaneously, which is essential for consistency in distributed systems.

Using Redis for Distributed Locking:

Redis can act as a distributed lock manager with minimal configuration.

1. **Install redis-py and redlock-py**:

```
pip install redis redlock-py
```

271

2. **Create a Distributed Lock**:

```python
from redis import Redis
from redlock import Redlock

redis_conn = Redis()
lock_manager = Redlock([redis_conn])

# Acquire lock
lock = lock_manager.lock("resource_name", 1000)  # Lock for 1000 ms
if lock:
    # Do work here
    lock_manager.unlock(lock)  # Release lock
```

Using Zookeeper for Distributed Locking:

Zookeeper provides distributed coordination, including lock management, in complex distributed applications.

- **Python Client**: Use kazoo library for interacting with Zookeeper.

```python
from kazoo.client import KazooClient
zk = KazooClient(hosts='127.0.0.1:2181')
zk.start()

with zk.Lock("/lockpath", "client_id") as lock:
    # Critical section
    pass
```

Best Practices:

- **Set Expiry on Locks**: Prevent deadlocks by setting lock expiry times.

- **Consistency**: Use locks for operations that must be consistent across distributed nodes (e.g., inventory updates).

How Do You Use Caching Mechanisms (e.g., Redis, Memcached) to Improve Application Performance?

Caching improves application performance by storing frequently accessed data in memory, reducing the need to fetch from slower backends.

1. **Using Redis for Caching:**

   Redis is a fast, in-memory data store that supports complex data types, making it a popular choice for caching.

   ```
   import redis

   # Connect to Redis
   client = redis.StrictRedis(host='localhost', port=6379, db=0)

   # Set and get cache
   client.set('key', 'value', ex=60)  # Set key with expiry of 60
   seconds
   value = client.get('key')
   print(value.decode())  # Outputs: value
   ```

2. **Using Memcached for Lightweight Caching:**

   Memcached is another in-memory cache, suited for simple, lightweight caching needs.

   - **Install python-memcached:**

     ```
     pip install python-memcached
     ```

   - **Set Up Cache:**

     ```
     import memcache
     client = memcache.Client([('127.0.0.1', 11211)])

     client.set('key', 'value', time=60)
     print(client.get('key'))  # Outputs: value
     ```

Use Cases:

- **Session Caching**: Store session data to avoid repetitive database queries.

- **API Caching**: Cache frequently requested data, such as API responses.

How Do You Handle Fault Tolerance and Retry Logic in Distributed Python Applications?

Fault tolerance ensures that applications continue to function in case of failures, while retry logic allows automatic re-attempts for failed tasks.

1. **Retry Mechanisms with Celery:**

   Celery supports built-in retry logic for handling failures.

   ```python
   from celery import Celery

   app = Celery('tasks', broker='redis://localhost:6379/0')

   @app.task(bind=True, max_retries=3)
   def my_task(self):
       try:
           # Simulated task
           pass
       except Exception as e:
           self.retry(countdown=5, exc=e)  # Retry after 5 seconds
   ```

2. **Implementing Exponential Backoff with tenacity:**

   Tenacity is a Python library for retrying code with customizable backoff strategies.

   - **Install Tenacity:**

     ```
     pip install tenacity
     ```

   - **Implement Exponential Backoff:**

     ```python
     from tenacity import retry, wait_exponential

     @retry(wait=wait_exponential(multiplier=1, min=4, max=10))
     def unreliable_task():
         # Task code here
         pass
     ```

Best Practices:

- **Log Failures**: Log each failure for monitoring and troubleshooting.

- **Set Limits**: Define maximum retries to avoid endless retry loops

How Do You Scale Python Applications Across Multiple Servers Using Load Balancing?

Load balancing distributes requests across multiple servers to handle increased traffic and prevent server overload.

1. **Using NGINX as a Load Balancer:**

   NGINX can be configured as a reverse proxy and load balancer for Python applications.

   - **Install NGINX**:

     ```
     sudo apt install nginx
     ```

   - **Configure NGINX for Load Balancing**:

     Add this configuration to the NGINX config file (/etc/nginx/nginx.conf).

     ```
     http {
         upstream myapp {
             server app1.example.com;
             server app2.example.com;
         }
         server {
             listen 80;
             location / {
                 proxy_pass http://myapp;
             }
         }
     }
     ```

   - **Restart NGINX**:

     ```
     sudo systemctl restart nginx
     ```

2. **Using Cloud Load Balancers (AWS ELB, Google Cloud LB):**

   Cloud providers offer managed load balancers that automatically scale with demand.

   - **AWS Elastic Load Balancing (ELB)**: Distributes incoming traffic to multiple EC2 instances.

   - **Google Cloud Load Balancer**: Scales across regions, handling global traffic

Best Practices:

- **Health Checks**: Configure health checks to route traffic only to healthy instances.

- **Session Persistence**: Use session persistence if needed to ensure users are routed to the same server during a session.

How Do You Use Service Discovery and Coordination Tools (e.g., Zookeeper, Consul) in Python Distributed Systems?

Service discovery tools help manage the dynamic nature of distributed services, while coordination tools ensure consistency and fault tolerance.

1. **Using Consul for Service Discovery:**

   Consul helps services discover each other and register themselves dynamically.

   - **Install Consul**: Follow the Consul installation guide for setup.

   - **Register a Service**: Use Python's requests library to register services with Consul.

   ```python
   import requests

   service_data = {
       "Name": "my-service",
       "Address": "127.0.0.1",
       "Port": 5000
   }
   requests.put('http://localhost:8500/v1/agent/service/register', json=service_data)
   ```

2. **Using Zookeeper for Coordination:**

   Zookeeper manages distributed synchronization and coordination.

   - **Install Kazoo**:

   ```
   pip install kazoo
   ```

   - **Connect and Use Zookeeper**:

   ```python
   from kazoo.client import KazooClient
   zk = KazooClient(hosts='127.0.0.1:2181')
   ```

```
zk.start()
# Create a node
zk.create("/my_service", b"service_data")
# Check existence
if zk.exists("/my_service"):
    print("Service node exists")
zk.stop()
```

Use Cases:

- **Dynamic Scaling**: Services can be discovered and load balanced automatically as new instances are added.

- **Leader Election**: Coordinate which instance acts as the leader in distributed systems.

Best Practices:

- **Cluster Management**: Run Consul or Zookeeper in a cluster mode for high availability.

- **Security**: Secure connections and communications between services using TLS.

Appendices

Appendix A: Useful Resources for Python Developers

Recommended Python Books

1. **"Fluent Python" by Luciano Ramalho**

   ○ *Overview*: This book delves deeply into Python's advanced features, offering insights into data structures, functions, and object-oriented programming.

   ○ *Best For*: Intermediate to advanced Python developers looking to deepen their understanding of Python's core features and idiomatic practices.

2. **"Effective Python" by Brett Slatkin**

   ○ *Overview*: This book offers 90 actionable tips and best practices to improve your Python code. It covers topics like performance optimization, Pythonic practices, and more.

   ○ *Best For*: Developers of all levels who want practical guidance for writing better Python code.

3. **"Python Crash Course" by Eric Matthes**

   ○ *Overview*: This beginner-friendly book provides a comprehensive introduction to Python, with hands-on projects including web applications and data visualization.

   ○ *Best For*: Beginners who want to build a strong foundation in Python and work on practical projects.

4. **"Automate the Boring Stuff with Python" by Al Sweigart**

   ○ *Overview*: A hands-on guide for automating everyday tasks like web scraping, data entry, and file manipulation.

   ○ *Best For*: Beginners to intermediate developers interested in practical automation.

5. **"Python Cookbook" by David Beazley and Brian K. Jones**

   ○ *Overview*: A collection of recipes for solving a wide range of common programming problems in Python, with explanations on how they work.

   ○ *Best For*: Experienced developers looking for quick solutions and deeper understanding of Python problems.

280

Best Python Online Courses and Certifications

1. **Coursera – "Python for Everybody" by Dr. Charles Severance**

   - *Description*: A comprehensive beginner's course covering Python basics, data structures, and networked application program interfaces.

   - *Certification*: Yes, with a Coursera subscription.

   - *Best For*: Absolute beginners who want a solid start.

2. **Udemy – "Complete Python Bootcamp: From Zero to Hero in Python" by Jose Portilla**

   - *Description*: A top-rated course with in-depth video lectures, coding exercises, and projects covering Python basics to advanced topics.

   - *Certification*: Yes, upon completion.

   - *Best For*: Developers looking for structured learning with practical projects.

3. **edX – "Introduction to Computer Science and Programming Using Python" (MITx)**

   - *Description*: This course from MIT focuses on Python fundamentals and algorithmic thinking.

   - *Certification*: Yes, with a fee.

   - *Best For*: Intermediate learners wanting to learn Python through an academic lens.

4. **Pluralsight – "Advanced Python"**

   - *Description*: Offers courses on specific advanced Python topics, including concurrency, data science, and performance optimization.

   - *Certification*: Available for course completion.

   - *Best For*: Intermediate to advanced developers.

5. **Codecademy – "Learn Python 3"**

   - *Description*: Interactive, hands-on lessons with projects to solidify Python 3 concepts.

   - *Best For*: Beginners to intermediate developers who prefer interactive learning.

Popular Python Blogs, Podcasts, and Newsletters

Blogs

- **Real Python**: In-depth tutorials, code examples, and practical Python tips. It covers everything from basic to advanced topics.

- **Python Software Foundation Blog**: Updates and insights from the Python core team.

- **Towards Data Science (Python Section)**: Articles on Python-related data science projects and best practices.

Podcasts

- **"Talk Python to Me"**: Interviews and stories from Python developers and enthusiasts, covering industry trends and project insights.

- **"Python Bytes"**: Quick summaries of Python news, packages, and tips.

- **"The Real Python Podcast"**: Hosted by the Real Python team, discussing Python programming and community trends.

Newsletters

- **Python Weekly**: A well-curated collection of Python news, tutorials, and packages delivered weekly.

- **PyCoder's Weekly**: A mix of Python news, library updates, and developer tools.

- **Real Python Newsletter**: Regular updates on new tutorials and articles from the Real Python site.

Essential GitHub Repositories for Python Developers

1. **The Algorithms – Python**: A comprehensive collection of algorithms implemented in Python, useful for learning and reference.

   https://github.com/TheAlgorithms/Python

2. **Awesome Python**: A curated list of awesome Python frameworks, libraries, software, and resources.

   https://github.com/vinta/awesome-python

3. **Python Patterns**: A repository showcasing Python design patterns and idiomatic Python code examples.

https://github.com/faif/python-patterns

4. **Scikit-learn**: The main repository for the popular machine learning library, with a vast collection of examples and documentation.

https://github.com/scikit-learn/scikit-learn

5. **Django**: The official repository for the Django web framework, ideal for those interested in web development.

https://github.com/django/django

Python Communities and Forums

1. **Reddit**:

   - **r/learnpython**: A supportive community for Python learners, ideal for questions and learning resources.

   - **r/Python**: General Python discussions, news, and updates.

2. **Stack Overflow**:

   - *Overview*: A go-to platform for asking questions and finding answers to Python-related problems.

   - *Best For*: Developers needing quick, reliable solutions to coding issues.

3. **Python Discord**:

   - *Description*: A large, active community with channels for learning Python, debugging code, and general Python discussion.

   - *Best For*: Real-time discussions and finding study groups or mentorship.

4. **Dev.to (Python Tag)**:

   - *Description*: Developers share articles, tutorials, and insights under the Python tag.

   - *Best For*: Staying updated on trends and learning through community-written articles.

5. **Hackerspaces and Meetup Groups**:

   - *Suggestion*: Join local or virtual Python meetups to engage with like-minded developers, share knowledge, and build projects collaboratively.

Open-Source Python Projects to Contribute To

1. **Matplotlib**: A comprehensive library for creating static, animated, and interactive plots in Python. Contributions can range from documentation to new features.

   https://github.com/matplotlib/matplotlib

2. **Django**: One of the most popular Python web frameworks, accepting contributions for bug fixes, features, and documentation.

   https://github.com/django/django

3. **Pandas**: The go-to library for data analysis and manipulation. Contributing to pandas can help you understand advanced data handling.

   https://github.com/pandas-dev/pandas

4. **Scrapy**: An open-source framework for web scraping. Perfect for developers interested in web scraping and contributing new middleware or features.

   https://github.com/scrapy/scrapy

5. **Home Assistant**: An open-source platform for home automation. Contributions can include integrations for new smart devices.

   https://github.com/home-assistant/core

6. **PyTorch**: A popular machine learning library used for deep learning research and production. Contributions often involve new models, tools, or bug fixes.

   https://github.com/pytorch/pytorch

Tips for Contributing:

- **Read Contribution Guidelines**: Each project typically has a CONTRIBUTING.md file with instructions.

- **Start with Documentation**: Contributing to documentation helps you understand the project and is a great starting point.

- **Join Project Discussions**: Participate in issues or discussions to learn what improvements are needed and how you can help.

Appendix B: Sample Python Projects and Case Studies

Building a Flask Web Application With Authentication and RESTful API

Overview:

Develop a web application using Flask with user authentication and RESTful API endpoints. This project helps you understand backend development, user management, and secure API creation.

Key Steps:

1. **Set Up Flask**:

```python
from flask import Flask, request, jsonify, render_template
from flask_sqlalchemy import SQLAlchemy
from flask_bcrypt import Bcrypt
from flask_jwt_extended import JWTManager, create_access_token

app = Flask(__name__)
app.config['SQLALCHEMY_DATABASE_URI'] = 'sqlite:///users.db'
app.config['JWT_SECRET_KEY'] = 'your_secret_key'
db = SQLAlchemy(app)
bcrypt = Bcrypt(app)
jwt = JWTManager(app)
```

2. **Create User Model and Authentication Logic**:

```python
class User(db.Model):
    id = db.Column(db.Integer, primary_key=True)
    username = db.Column(db.String(80), unique=True,
nullable=False)
    password = db.Column(db.String(200), nullable=False)

@app.route('/register', methods=['POST'])
def register():
    data = request.get_json()
    hashed_password =
bcrypt.generate_password_hash(data['password']).decode('utf-8')
```

285

```python
    new_user = User(username=data['username'],
password=hashed_password)
    db.session.add(new_user)
    db.session.commit()
    return jsonify({"message": "User registered successfully!"})

@app.route('/login', methods=['POST'])
def login():
    data = request.get_json()
    user = User.query.filter_by(username=data['username']).first()
    if user and bcrypt.check_password_hash(user.password,
data['password']):
        access_token = create_access_token(identity={'username':
user.username})
        return jsonify(access_token=access_token)
    return jsonify({"message": "Invalid credentials"}), 401
```

3. **Run the Application**:
   ```
   flask run
   ```

Outcome:

A web application with user registration and login, showcasing how to secure routes and provide API access tokens.

Developing a Machine Learning Pipeline Using scikit-learn and pandas

Overview:

Create a pipeline that loads data, preprocesses it, trains a model, and evaluates its performance.

Key Steps:

1. **Load and Preprocess Data**:

```python
import pandas as pd
from sklearn.model_selection import train_test_split
from sklearn.preprocessing import StandardScaler
from sklearn.pipeline import Pipeline
from sklearn.linear_model import LogisticRegression
from sklearn.metrics import accuracy_score
```

286

```
df = pd.read_csv('dataset.csv')
X = df.drop('target', axis=1)
y = df['target']

X_train, X_test, y_train, y_test = train_test_split(X, y,
test_size=0.3, random_state=42)
```

2. **Create the Pipeline**:

```
pipeline = Pipeline([
    ('scaler', StandardScaler()),
    ('classifier', LogisticRegression())
])

pipeline.fit(X_train, y_train)
y_pred = pipeline.predict(X_test)
print("Accuracy:", accuracy_score(y_test, y_pred))
```

Outcome:

A functional ML pipeline demonstrating data preprocessing, model training, and evaluation.

Automating AWS Infrastructure Using Python and Boto3

Overview:

Use **Boto3** to automate AWS tasks such as creating EC2 instances, S3 buckets, and managing security groups.

Key Steps:

1. **Install and Configure Boto3**:

```
pip install boto3
```

2. **Create and Launch an EC2 Instance**:

```
import boto3

ec2 = boto3.resource('ec2')

instance = ec2.create_instances(
```

```
        ImageId='ami-0abcdef1234567890',
        MinCount=1,
        MaxCount=1,
        InstanceType='t2.micro',
        KeyName='your-key-pair'
    )
    print("Instance ID:", instance[0].id)
```

3. **Create an S3 Bucket**:

```
s3 = boto3.client('s3')
s3.create_bucket(Bucket='my-automated-bucket')
```

Outcome:

A script that automates infrastructure tasks, simplifying cloud management.

Designing a Data Pipeline for Real-Time Data Processing Using Kafka and pandas

Overview:

Design a pipeline to read, process, and analyze streaming data in real-time using **Kafka** and **pandas**.

Key Steps:

1. **Set Up Kafka and Install kafka-python**:

```
pip install kafka-python
```

2. **Produce and Consume Messages**:

```
from kafka import KafkaProducer, KafkaConsumer
import pandas as pd
# Producer
producer = KafkaProducer(bootstrap_servers='localhost:9092')
producer.send('data_topic', b'{"temperature": 23, "humidity": 60}')

# Consumer
consumer = KafkaConsumer('data_topic',
bootstrap_servers='localhost:9092')
```

```
for msg in consumer:
    data = pd.read_json(msg.value)
    print(data)
```

Outcome:

A real-time data pipeline that processes and prints streaming data, demonstrating the integration of Kafka and pandas.

Creating a Scalable Microservice Using Flask and Docker

Overview:

Develop a scalable microservice with Flask and containerize it using Docker for easy deployment.

Key Steps:

1. **Create a Simple Flask App:**

```python
from flask import Flask

app = Flask(__name__)

@app.route('/')
def home():
    return "Hello, this is a scalable microservice!"

if __name__ == '__main__':
    app.run(host='0.0.0.0', port=5000)
```

1. **Dockerize the Flask Application:**

    ○ Create a Dockerfile:

```dockerfile
FROM python:3.8-slim
WORKDIR /app
COPY . /app
RUN pip install flask
CMD ["python", "app.py"]
```

- Build and run the container:

```
docker build -t flask-microservice .
docker run -p 5000:5000 flask-microservice
```

Outcome:

A Dockerized microservice that can be deployed and scaled across multiple containers

Implementing a Web Scraping Tool Using BeautifulSoup and requests

Overview:

Create a web scraper to extract and parse data from web pages using **BeautifulSoup** and **requests**.

Key Steps:

1. **Install the Required Libraries**:

```
pip install beautifulsoup4 requests
```

2. **Write the Web Scraper**:

```python
from bs4 import BeautifulSoup
import requests

url = 'https://example.com'
response = requests.get(url)
soup = BeautifulSoup(response.content, 'html.parser')

# Extract specific data
titles = soup.find_all('h2')
for title in titles:
    print(title.text)
```

Outcome:

A tool that extracts data from websites and displays it, showcasing the basics of web scraping

.

Deploying a Deep Learning Model Using TensorFlow, Flask, and Docker

Overview:

Deploy a pre-trained deep learning model with **TensorFlow**, serve it with **Flask**, and containerize the application using **Docker**.

Key Steps:

1. **Load and Serve the Model with Flask**:

```python
from flask import Flask, request, jsonify
import tensorflow as tf
app = Flask(__name__)
model = tf.keras.models.load_model('my_model.h5')
@app.route('/predict', methods=['POST'])
def predict():
    data = request.get_json()
    input_data = tf.convert_to_tensor([data['features']])
    prediction = model.predict(input_data)
    return jsonify({'prediction': prediction.tolist()})
if __name__ == '__main__':
    app.run(host='0.0.0.0', port=5000)
```

2. **Dockerize the Flask Application**:

   - Create a Dockerfile:

```dockerfile
FROM python:3.8-slim
WORKDIR /app
COPY . /app
RUN pip install flask tensorflow
CMD ["python", "app.py"]
```

   - Build and run the Docker container:

```
docker build -t deep-learning-api .
docker run -p 5000:5000 deep-learning-api
```

Outcome:

A containerized Flask application serving a TensorFlow model, making it accessible via RESTful API for predictions.

Appendix C: Preparing for a Python Developer Interview

Common Python Interview Mistakes to Avoid

Not Following Pythonic Practices:

- **Mistake**: Writing code that is syntactically correct but not idiomatic or "Pythonic."

- **Solution**: Use list comprehensions, follow naming conventions, and use built-in functions and modules when appropriate (e.g., sum(), zip(), enumerate()).

Overusing Global Variables:

- **Mistake**: Using global variables can lead to unexpected behavior and make debugging difficult.

- **Solution**: Prefer function arguments and return values for data manipulation.

Ignoring Edge Cases:

- **Mistake**: Not accounting for edge cases like empty lists, single-element lists, or special characters.

- **Solution**: Always test your functions with edge cases.

Inefficient Code:

- **Mistake**: Writing code with poor time and space complexity.

- **Solution**: Use data structures and algorithms that optimize performance, such as sets for membership tests or dictionaries for key-value lookups.

How to Tackle Algorithm and Data Structure Problems in Python

Understand the Problem Thoroughly:

- **Tip**: Clarify the problem statement and ask questions if anything is unclear.

- **Example**: If the problem involves finding duplicates in a list, ask if there are memory or time constraints.

Plan Before Coding:

- **Tip**: Spend a few minutes brainstorming the approach and writing down pseudocode or an outline before starting to code.

Choose the Right Data Structures:

- **Example**: Use a **set** for fast membership checks or a **deque** from collections for efficient append and pop operations.

Focus on Time and Space Complexity:

- **Example**: Use $O(n \log n)$ algorithms (e.g., sorted()) instead of $O(n^2)$ when handling large datasets.

Use Python Libraries:

- **Tip**: Leverage built-in libraries like collections, itertools, and heapq to simplify your solution.

Sample Problem:

- **Question**: Find the top k frequent elements in a list.

- **Approach**:

```python
from collections import Counter
import heapq

def top_k_frequent(nums, k):
    count = Counter(nums)
    return heapq.nlargest(k, count.keys(), key=count.get)
```

Best Practices for Explaining Python Code in Interviews

Use Clear and Concise Language:

- **Tip**: Clearly explain what each part of your code does and why you chose that approach.

- **Example**: "I used a set here because it allows $O(1)$ average time complexity for lookups."

Walk Through Your Code Step-by-Step:

- **Tip**: Narrate how your code works with a simple example input.

- **Example**: "Given the list [1, 2, 3, 2, 4], my code initializes a set and iterates through the list, adding each unique number…"

Mention Edge Cases:

- **Tip**: Show the interviewer that you considered different edge cases and how your code handles them.

- **Example**: "This code handles edge cases like an empty list by returning an empty result set."

Discuss Trade-Offs:

- **Tip**: If there's more than one way to solve the problem, explain why you chose your solution over another.

- **Example**: "I used a dictionary to store counts because it provides $O(1)$ insertion and retrieval time, which is optimal for this use case."

Tips for Solving Whiteboard and Coding Challenge Problems

Practice with Mock Interviews:

- **Tip**: Practice on platforms like LeetCode, HackerRank, or with peers to simulate real interview conditions.

Start with a Simple Solution:

- **Tip**: Begin with a basic solution to ensure you understand the problem, then optimize as needed.

Communicate Continuously:

- **Tip**: Speak aloud as you code, explaining your thought process. This helps interviewers understand your approach and gives them opportunities to guide you if necessary.

Manage Your Time Effectively:

- **Tip**: Allocate time wisely for reading the problem, brainstorming, coding, and testing.

Write Clean and Readable Code:

- **Tip**: Follow PEP 8 guidelines, use meaningful variable names, and add comments where necessary.

How to Showcase Python Projects and Contributions in Interviews

Prepare a Portfolio of Your Best Projects:

- **Tip**: Include projects that demonstrate a range of skills, such as web development, data analysis, or automation.

- **Example**: A Flask app with authentication, a machine learning pipeline in scikit-learn, or a web scraper using BeautifulSoup.

Highlight Your Role and Contributions:

- **Tip**: Emphasize the specific tasks you performed and any unique challenges you overcame.

- **Example**: "In my machine learning project, I optimized the model's performance by implementing a grid search for hyperparameter tuning."

Prepare for Technical Questions on Your Projects:

- **Tip**: Be ready to explain your code, libraries used, and why you made certain design choices.

- **Example**: "I used pandas for data manipulation because it handles large datasets efficiently and provides powerful data analysis tools."

Include Code Samples in Your Portfolio:

- **Tip**: Share a GitHub link or a code snippet that shows off your coding style and problem-solving abilities.

Behavioral and Leadership Questions for Senior Python Developers

Common Behavioral Questions:

- **"Tell me about a time you led a project."**

- **"How do you handle conflicts within your team?"**

- **"Describe a challenge you faced and how you overcame it."**

Preparing STAR-Format Answers:

- **Situation**: Briefly describe the context.

- **Task**: Explain your responsibility.

- **Action**: Detail what you did to handle the situation.

- **Result**: Share the outcome and any learnings.

Example Answer:

- **Question**: "Tell me about a time when you improved a process."

- **Answer**:

  - **Situation**: "Our deployment process was manual and error-prone."

  - **Task**: "As the team lead, I was responsible for streamlining the process."

  - **Action**: "I implemented a CI/CD pipeline using Jenkins and Docker to automate deployments."

  - **Result**: "Deployment time was reduced by 50%, and the process became more reliable."

Emphasize Leadership and Mentorship:

- **Tip**: Highlight any mentoring roles or how you have helped junior developers grow.

- **Example**: "I organized weekly code reviews and training sessions to ensure best practices were followed across the team."

Preparing for Pair Programming and Live Coding Interviews

Practice Collaborative Coding:

- **Tip**: Practice pair programming with peers or participate in coding challenges that involve real-time collaboration.

Familiarize Yourself with Interview Platforms:

- **Tip**: Platforms like CoderPad, HackerRank, and LeetCode often simulate real-time coding interviews. Ensure you know the basic functions and shortcuts of these platforms.

Stay Calm and Seek Clarification:

- **Tip**: If you're unsure of the requirements, ask questions rather than making assumptions.

Communicate Clearly During Coding:

- **Tip**: Explain your code as you write it to show your logical thought process and engage the interviewer in your approach.

Handle Feedback Positively:

- **Tip**: Be open to suggestions and incorporate interviewer feedback to show adaptability and a willingness to learn.

296

Plan Before You Code:

- **Tip**: Outline your plan or pseudocode to structure your solution, even if you're coding live.

Example Question for Practice:

- **"Implement a function that reverses a linked list."**

- **Approach**:

```python
class ListNode:
    def __init__(self, value=0, next=None):
        self.value = value
        self.next = next

def reverse_linked_list(head):
    prev = None
    current = head
    while current:
        next_node = current.next
        current.next = prev
        prev = current
        current = next_node
    return prev
```

Outcome:

Your ability to handle live coding challenges showcases your confidence, communication skills, and proficiency in Python programming.

Appendix D: Glossary of Python Terms

Core Python Concepts

- **List Comprehensions**: A concise way to create lists using a single line of code.

  Example: [x**2 for x in range(10) if x % 2 == 0] creates a list of squares of even numbers.

- **Iterators**: Objects that allow you to iterate over collections like lists or strings using the __iter__() and __next__() methods.

Example: Using iter() and next() to loop through an iterable manually.

- **Generators**: Special types of iterators created using functions with the yield keyword to produce a sequence of values lazily.

```
def countdown(n):
    while n > 0:
        yield n
        n -= 1
```

- **Decorators**: Functions that modify the behavior of other functions or methods. They use the @decorator_name syntax.

```
def my_decorator(func):
    def wrapper():
        print("Before function runs")
        func()
        print("After function runs")
    return wrapper


@my_decorator
def say_hello():
    print("Hello!")
```

- **Context Managers**: Used to manage resources efficiently with with statements, ensuring proper cleanup.

Example: Using with open('file.txt', 'r') as f: to read a file safely.

Key OOP Terms

- **Polymorphism**: The ability of different objects to be accessed through the same interface, typically achieved through method overriding.

Example: Different classes having a method called speak(), where each class implements it differently.

- **Inheritance**: A mechanism to create a new class from an existing class, inheriting attributes and methods.

```
class Animal:
    def speak(self):
```

```
        pass

class Dog(Animal):
    def speak(self):
        return "Woof!"
```

- **Encapsulation**: The concept of restricting access to certain components of an object to protect the integrity of its data.

  Example: Using private variables prefixed with _ or __ (e.g., __private_var).

- **Abstraction**: Hiding implementation details and showing only the necessary functionality.

  Example: Abstract base classes defined using the abc module.

Python Libraries and Frameworks

- **Flask**: A lightweight web framework for building web applications quickly and easily.

- **Django**: A high-level web framework that encourages rapid development and clean, pragmatic design.

- **NumPy**: A library for numerical computations in Python, providing support for arrays and matrix operations.

- **pandas**: A data analysis library offering data structures and operations for manipulating numerical tables and time series.

- **requests**: A user-friendly library for making HTTP requests in Python.

- **BeautifulSoup**: A library for parsing HTML and XML documents, useful for web scraping.

- **scikit-learn**: A library for machine learning, providing simple and efficient tools for data analysis and modeling.

Testing and Debugging Terminology

- **Mocking**: The practice of creating a simulated version of an object or method to test code in isolation.

  Example: Using unittest.mock to replace parts of code for testing.

- **Fixtures**: Predefined setups for test environments used to create consistent test data and states.

  Example: Fixtures in pytest allow you to create reusable test configurations.

299

- **Test Coverage**: A metric indicating the percentage of code that is executed during testing.

  Tool Example: coverage.py helps track code coverage in Python projects.

- **Breakpoint**: A debugging tool used to pause code execution at a specific point to inspect variables and code flow.

- **Assertion**: A statement used to check if a condition in the code returns True, ensuring expected behavior in tests.

  Example: assert x == 5

Asynchronous Programming Terms

- **Event Loop**: The core of asynchronous programming that continually checks for and executes tasks when they are ready.

  Example: Python's asyncio.get_event_loop() creates and manages event loops.

- **Coroutine**: A function defined with async def that can be paused and resumed, enabling asynchronous behavior.

```
async def my_coroutine():
    await asyncio.sleep(1)
    print("Done!")
```

- **Future**: Represents a value that will be available at some point. Used to handle the result of an asynchronous operation.

- **await**: A keyword that pauses the execution of an async function until the awaited task is complete.

  Example: await asyncio.sleep(2)

- **async/await Syntax**: The combination used to write asynchronous code that is readable and non-blocking.

<u>Memory and Performance Profiling Tools</u>

- **cProfile**: A built-in Python module for profiling that provides detailed reports on function calls, execution time, and more.

  Example: cProfile.run('my_function()')

- **tracemalloc**: A module to trace memory allocation and identify memory leaks.

```python
import tracemalloc
tracemalloc.start()
# Code to profile
snapshot = tracemalloc.take_snapshot()
```

- **line_profiler**: A tool to profile the memory usage of Python code line by line.

- **memory_profiler**: A module that helps measure memory usage in Python.

  Example: @profile decorator to monitor memory in functions.

Security Terminology in Python

- **CSRF (Cross-Site Request Forgery)**: An attack that tricks the victim into submitting unwanted actions on a web application where they are authenticated.

  Prevention: Use CSRF tokens in forms.

- **SQL Injection**: A code injection technique that exploits vulnerabilities in an application's software by inserting malicious SQL queries.

  Prevention: Use parameterized queries and ORMs.

- **XSS (Cross-Site Scripting)**: A vulnerability where attackers inject malicious scripts into content delivered to users.

  Prevention: Sanitize and escape user input properly.

- **Hashing and Encryption**: Techniques used to secure data. Hashing is irreversible (e.g., password hashing), while encryption can be decrypted with a key.

- **JWT (JSON Web Token)**: A compact, URL-safe means of representing claims transferred between two parties, commonly used for securing API endpoints.

About the Author

Konstantin Ryabichenko is a developer and technology leader with more than 12 years of experience in the FinTech software industry. Throughout his career, Konstantin has progressed from a junior developer to the head of development and Chief Technology Officer. His professional experience includes managing large IT teams, developing technology strategies, and successfully launching large-scale projects.

Konstantin is actively involved in the development of modern solutions, such as cryptocurrency processing systems and online payment platforms that process thousands of transactions daily. His key strengths include system architecture design, working with microservices, process automation, and deep knowledge of security (PCI DSS, OWASP).

Konstantin started writing this book to share his knowledge and practical experience, aiming to help other developers not only pass technical interviews but also better understand the principles of modern web application development. He believes that every developer, regardless of their level, can achieve success if they continuously learn and improve.

Outside of work, Konstantin is interested in new technologies, cryptocurrencies, and is always open to new professional challenges.

You can reach Konstantin Ryabichenko at:

- **Email**: k.ryabichenko@gmail.com

- **LinkedIn**: linkedin.com/in/ryabichenko-konstantin